Canadian Concepts 3

Lynda Berish
Sandra Thibaudeau

Prentice Hall Canada Inc., Scarborough, Ontario

Canadian Cataloguing in Publication Data

Berish, Lynda, 1952–
Canadian concepts 3

ISBN 0-13-117060-0

1. English language – Textbooks for second
language learners.* 2. English language – Grammar –
1950– . 3. English language – Grammar –
Problems, exercises, etc. I. Thibaudeau,
Sandra, 1943– . II. Title.

PE1128.B47 1992   428.2'4   C92-093527-3

Prentice-Hall, Inc., Englewood Cliffs, New Jersey
Prentice-Hall International, Inc., London
Prentice-Hall of Australia, Pty., Ltd., Sydney
Prentice-Hall of India Pvt., Ltd., New Delhi
Prentice-Hall of Japan, Inc., Tokyo
Prentice-Hall of Southeast Asia (Pte.) Ltd., Singapore
Editora Prentice-Hall do Brasil Ltda., Rio de Janeiro
Prentice-Hall Hispanoamericana, S.A., Mexico

ISBN 0-13-117060-0

Acquisitions editor: Marjorie Walker
Developmental editor: Linda Gorman
Production editor: Elynor Kagan
Production coordinator: Lisa Kreuch
Design and layout: Joseph Chin
Illustrations: Peter Grau, Stephen Taylor
Cover design: Aurora Di Ciaula
Cover illustration: June Bradford

2 3 4 5 WL 96 95 94 93

Printed and bound in Canada by Webcom Limited

Contents

To the Teacher

The *Canadian Concepts* Series

The *Canadian Concepts* Series is a six-book series designed for students learning English in Canada. Survival topics and cultural information based on Canadian themes help students integrate into the community. These themes are recycled with increasing complexity throughout the series. Practical topics in the lower levels progress to topics of interest and concern to more advanced students.

The *Canadian Concepts* Series is communicative in approach. The method offers productive strategies for language learning based on student-centred interaction. The pedagogical model presents students with challenging input, and provides activities that involve the students in information exchange. Students are often asked to work in pairs or groups to extend their understanding through interaction. Fluency activities are supported with spelling, dictation, pronunciation and writing tasks that focus on accuracy.

Canadian Concepts 3

Students using *Canadian Concepts 3* are challenged by richer and more complex input that recycles familiar themes and mixes survival topics with general information. Students are asked to participate in situations that are less structured than those in *Canadian Concepts 2,* and they begin to generate more language to explain and express opinions.

Students gain the confidence to function in English from the survival topics and cultural information, and are motivated to use their new skills in the real world through the Community Contact Tasks.

Teachers and students will appreciate the simplicity of the materials. Clear illustrations provide visual support and stimulate student discussion. Worksheets for some activities are provided in a special section of the Teacher's Manual, with permission to photocopy.

The Units

Canadian Concepts 3 is divided into 15 self-contained units. The units focus on survival topics and themes that are relevant to the students.

Each unit begins with an overview of topics and activities. The unit is then made up of a variety of activities that follow a basic three-part pattern. The first section introduces the subject. The next section calls for students to work with challenging material in the core reading or listening activity. Then the language is reviewed in a variety of ways.

The Activities

The "Get Ready" section provides reading or listening preparation. These pre-activities introduce the topic and generate interest in a variety of ways: through prediction exercises, discussion questions, dictation or interaction based on illustrations. The Teacher's Manual provides suggestions for warm-up activities to do before students open their books.

Core activities focus on taped passages or reading texts. They promote strategies of guessing from context, trying out possible answers and revising understanding through successive steps. Core activities consist of a variety of tasks: reading or listening for general information, reading or listening for detailed information, and listening for sounds.

Follow-up activities recycle language in the unit, providing an opportunity for students to express themselves and use new vocabulary. They include discussion activities, opportunities to practise language, vocabulary review, grammar review and writing.

Pre-Activities	Core Activities	Review and Recycle	Real-Life Application
Get Ready to Read	Read for General Ideas	Review Vocabulary	Role Play
Get Ready to Listen	Read for Details	Review Expressions	Exchange Information
Get Ready to Discuss	Read to Increase Speed	Practise Speaking	What About You?
	Listen for Meaning	Practise Grammar	Tell the Story
	Listen for Details	Practise Writing	Express Yourself
	Listen for Sounds	Practise Numbers	Community Contact Tasks
		Transfer Information	
		Use Information	
		Dictations	
		Practise Spelling	
		Crossword Puzzles	

Key to Symbols

○ ○	Listening Activity	□ □	Work with a Partner
📖	Reading Activity	□□ / □□	Work in a Group
✏	Writing Activity	🎭	Role Play

Listening Programme

The listening programme in *Canadian Concepts 3* consists of survival English dialogues and short listening passages. Students listen to natural sounding Canadian English on topics relevant to their daily lives and activities. They are able to move through stages of comprehension as they listen first for general meaning, then for details and finally for sounds in reduced speech.

Teachers will appreciate that passages are recorded two or three times in sequence to avoid the need to rewind and hunt for material on the tape during class.

Complete listening scripts and answer keys are provided with the Teacher's Manual. Listening worksheets are included in the Teacher's Manual

Supplementary Grammar

Explanations of grammar points and practice exercises are provided in the Supplementary Grammar section. These exercises also review vocabulary from the preceding units. Suggestions for introducing grammar points are given in the Teacher's Manual.

Community Contact Tasks

The Community Contact Tasks are designed to complement activities done in class. They are linked to units in the book. Students have an opportunity to practise their English in real-life situations outside the classroom. A variety of tasks has been provided so that a selection can be made according to the needs and interests of the students in a particular class. Worksheets are provided in the Teacher's Manual.

Teacher's Manual

Each book in the series has its own Teacher's Manual that includes:

- step-by-step instructions keyed to the student's book;

- suggestions for classroom interaction;

- answers for exercises;

- tape scripts for listening activities;

– teacher's scripts for dictations and pronunciation exercises;

– student worksheets.

Detailed teacher's notes are included to make the intention of activities clear and to guide new teachers. Experienced teachers will find that the material lends itself to flexibility and accommodates individual teaching styles.

The authors wish success to their colleagues and the students who use these Canadian materials.

Lynda Berish
Sandra Thibaudeau

Acknowledgements

We would like to acknowledge the support and assistance of the following people in the classroom testing of the materials in this book: Maria De Rosa Wilson, Shelly Coleman, Dennis Plosker, Susan St. George, Sandra McLaren and Terrance Clark. Their valuable comments, support and suggestions have been much appreciated.

We would like to thank friends and family who have supported our efforts: our patient husbands, John Berish and Charles Gruss, and our hungry children, Tara and Andrea Berish and Jean-Baptiste, Gabrielle and Annabel Thibaudeau. We would like to thank Tara Berish and Jessica Dressler for their proofreading. We would also like to thank Howard Berish, Richard Goldman and Stephen Goldman for their advice, and Max and Millicent Goldman who, over many years and in many ways, have offered the kind of encouragement writers need to keep going.

We would like to express our sincere thanks to Elizabeth Taborek, from the Toronto Board, Continuing Education and Elisabeth Nadeau, Co-ordinator of ESL, Dorset Community College, for their enthusiastic responses to our materials.

We would also like to express appreciation to our reviewers, Carole Trépanier (English Language Institute, University of British Columbia), Audrey Bonham (Community College Extension Centre, Red River College) and Marian Hislop (Palmer Junior Secondary School) for their encouraging comments and suggestions.

The World

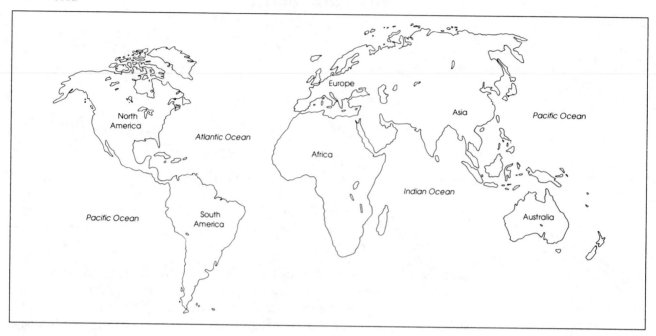

Canada

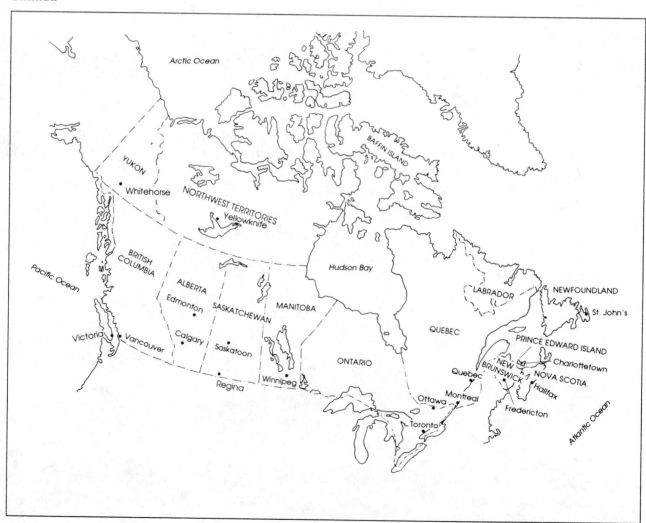

Names

What's Your Name?
Discussion

John Around the World
Interaction

Family Names
Reading

Names in Other Countries
Interaction

What's Your Name?

Discuss these questions in a group.

1. What is your first name?

2. What is your last name, or surname?

3. Do you have a middle name? What is it?

4. What does your name mean?

5. In your language, what are the most popular girls' names? What are the most popular boys' names? What are the most popular family names?

6. In your culture, do women change their names when they get married?

7. Do you have a nickname? What is it?

John Around the World

The name "John" is very common. It is a name used in many countries, but there are different ways to say it.

Match the version of John with the country to which it belongs.

Name	Country
Giovanni	Ireland
Hansel	France
Ivan	Morocco
Jean	Switzerland
Jan	Holland
Sean	Greece
Ioannes	Russia
Yahya	Italy
Johann	Austria

Family Names

Exercise 1: Get Ready to Read

Discuss these questions in a group.

1. What are some common last names in North America?
2. How do people get their names in North America?

Exercise 2: Read Quickly for General Ideas

Family Names

Where did you get your name? If you come from North America, you probably got your name from your family. Your first name was given to you by your parents, and your last name, or surname, is the same name that your parents have: your family name.

Long ago, however, people had only one name. A man could be called simply John or Peter. A woman could be called Mary or Elizabeth. After some time, there were many people with the same name, so second names were needed. A child took the father's name as a last name. In this way, the children of John were called, for example, Peter and Mary Johnson. Names such as Wilson (Will's son), Jackson, Anderson and Davidson came into use.

"Mac" or "Mc" means "son of," so the name MacGregor means son of Gregory, and MacDonald means son of Donald. "Fitz" is another way of saying "son of." **Fils** means "son" in French. So Fitzpatrick and Fitzgerald mean son, or child, of Patrick or Gerald.

Not all people got their names from their fathers. Some got their names from the places they lived in. For example, a family that lived in a village with many green trees and plants was called Green or Greenberg. If they lived in a town called Moor, they were called the Moores.

Sometimes people got their names from the way they looked. A tall person was, perhaps, called Long. If people in a family had dark hair, the family was sometimes called the Blacks or the Browns. If their hair was light, they may have been called the Whites.

People often took their names from the kind of work they did. A person who sewed clothing was named Taylor. Another person who baked bread was called Baker. A person who had a very good voice was named Singer.

After a while these names stayed with people and became family names that are still used today.

The Browns

Exercise 3: Read Carefully for Details

Work with a partner. Look in the text for the answers.

1. In North America, how do people get their first names? How do they get their last names?

2. Long ago, how many names did people have?

3. Why did people start to have more names?

4. How did people get their new names?

5. Give two examples of ways to write "son of."

6. Make a chart similar to the one below to show three ways people got their names. Give examples of each.

Ways to Get Name	Examples

Names in Other Countries

Discuss these questions in a group.

1. Are some family names in your language names of colours?

2. Are some names in your language names of flowers or fruits?

3. Are names sometimes names of animals?

4. Are names sometimes the names of jobs or trades?

5. Does your language add "son" or "daughter" to make names?

6. Does your language have names from nature?

7. What are some names in your language that have meanings?

The list of English names below may give you some ideas for your answers.

White

Brown

Black

Gray

Green

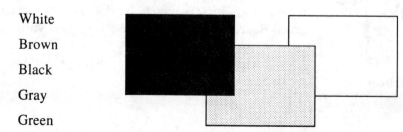

Fish
Bull
Trout
Fox
Bird

Johnson
Harrison
Benson
Williamson
Robertson

Taylor
Baker
Smith
Singer
Carpenter

Field
Bush
Forest
Rivers
Waters

Small Talk

Chatting
Reading
Cultural Information

What About You?
Discussion

Nice to Meet You
Listening Activity 1

Chatting

Exercise 1: Get Ready to Read

Work in a group to discuss these questions. When people in North America meet for the first time, some of these questions are polite and some are rude. Which questions are rude?

1. How old are you, Mrs. Brown?
2. Did you watch the hockey game on Saturday?
3. What do you do, Ted?
4. How many children do you have?
5. How much money do you make?
6. Why aren't you married yet?
7. Where does your wife work?
8. What is your religion?
9. Did you go away on holiday this year?
10. How much did you pay for your dress?
11. When are you going to have children?
12. What are you doing here?

Exercise 2: Read Carefully for Information

Read the text carefully. Then use the information in the text to check your answers to the questions.

Chatting

When people in North America meet for the first time, they do not talk about things that are personal. Some subjects are private and it is not polite to ask people about them. People talk about their families, but they don't talk about why they aren't married or why they don't have children.

The way you begin a conversation can be polite or impolite too. Try not to interrupt a person who is reading or working. If something is very important and you must interrupt, you can say, "Excuse me."

When two people meet in public, one doesn't ask questions about why the other person is there or what the other person is doing. These questions are not seen as friendly. They are probably seen as nosey.

People ask each other about their health, but it isn't polite to go into details. People often talk about their jobs, but they don't talk about their salaries. Safe topics include the weather, sports and holidays. Topics to avoid are politics, personal details and religion.

What About You?

Talk about the questions on page 7 again. In your culture, are they polite or rude questions?

Nice to Meet You

Listening Activity 1

Exercise 1: Get Ready to Listen

A. Work in a group. Look at the picture on page 9.

1. Where do you think these people are?

2. Name some polite topics that these people could talk about.

B. Read these questions aloud with a partner. What do you think the conversation will be about?

1. How many people are in the conversation?

   a) two

   b) three

   c) four

2. What is not true about Maria's job?

    a) It's in a high school.

    b) The students are young.

    c) She teaches adults.

3. Where does Amir work?

    a) in a dentist's office

    b) in a travel agency

    c) in an apartment

4. What is true about Amir and Nadia?

    a) They travel to work.

    b) They live downtown.

    c) They don't like their jobs.

5. Who works in a bank?

    a) Nadia

    b) Amir

    c) Maria

6. What does a bank teller do?

    a) cash cheques

    b) check the time

    c) deposit money

○○ Exercise 2: Listen for Meaning

Listen to the conversation. What is the conversation about?

○○ Exercise 3: Listen for Details

Go back to the questions. While you listen, choose the correct answers.

○○ Exercise 4: Listen for Sounds

While you listen, write the missing words.

Nice to Meet You

Maria: Hi, I'm Maria.

Nadia: Nice ____ meet you. I'm Nadia, and this is my husband Amir. What ____ you do, Maria?

Maria: ____ a teacher. I teach at the high school.

Nadia: Really. Do you like your job?

Maria: It's OK. The problem is ____ the students are very young. I prefer teaching adults. What do you do Amir?

Amir: I'm ____ dentist. I work in an office downtown. I don't really like travelling to work. Nadia works downtown too, so we have an apartment near our jobs.

Maria: Me too. I like ____ live near my work. What do you do Nadia?

Nadia: ____ a teller. I work at the National Bank. I like working with the public.

Maria: Yes. And all that money!

Nadia: Money, yes. But most of my job is just cashing cheques ____ making deposits. The money isn't mine.

Maria: Too bad, ha ha.

Amir: Well, nice talking to ____, Maria.

Maria: Yes, nice ____ meet you Amir, Nadia.

Exercise 5: Practise Speaking

Practise reading the dialogue with a partner. Then change roles and read it again.

Education

Education in the Past
Reading

First Schools in Canada
Listening Activity 2

What About You?
Discussion

My School
Writing

Education in the Past

Exercise 1: Get Ready to Read

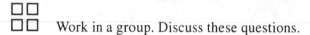

Work in a group. Discuss these questions.

1. What subjects do children study in school today?
2. What subjects did people study in the past?
3. Where were the first universities?

Exercise 2: Read Quickly for General Ideas

Education in the Past

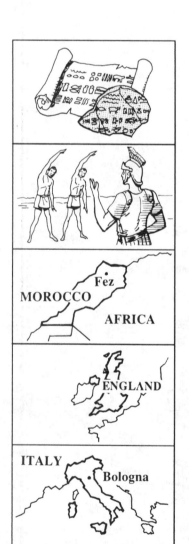

The first school in the history of the world was in Sumaria. It existed in about 3500 BC (before Christ). This was about 5500 years ago. In this school students learned to write. Their writing looked like small pictures. It was like the writing that people used in ancient Egypt.

The first schools in Egypt taught language and morals. In ancient India, schools taught language and they taught religion. Later they taught art and mathematics. Students in Greek schools learned many things. They learned to be brave and to be good citizens. They also learned music and dancing.

In Ancient Rome, only children from rich families were educated. Sometimes they had private teachers who came to their homes. They learned to write and do arithmetic. Keeping fit was important, so they learned wrestling and fencing.

The oldest school that is still open today is in the city of Fez in Morocco. It is the University of Karueein. It began in the year 859, and students can still study there.

The first university in Europe was in Italy. It was the University of Bologna, and it began in 1088. Oxford University in England began in 1167. It was the first university in England. These universities taught subjects such as law, medicine and mathematics.

In the United States, Harvard University is the oldest university. It started in 1636. The oldest university in Canada is Laval University. It started in 1663. The first English-speaking university in Canada was King's College. It became a university in 1789. Students still go to these universities today.

Many universities in Canada taught religion at first. Soon they began to teach other subjects as well. They taught agriculture, engineering, medicine, law, business and the arts.

Exercise 3: Transfer Information

Read the text carefully. Work with a partner to make a chart similar to the one below and fill in the information. Put an ✗ if you can't find the information in the text.

Year	Place	Name of School	Subjects
3500 BC	Sumaria	✗	writing
	Egypt		
	India		
			music, dancing, being good citizens
	Rome		
859			
		University of Bologna	
	England		
1636			
1663	Canada		
		King's College	

Exercise 4: Read Carefully for Details

Work with a partner. Look in the text for the answers.

1. Where did people use small pictures as writing?

2. Name two places where language was a school subject.

3. What subjects were added later in Indian schools?

4. What subjects did students in Greek schools learn?

5. Which children were educated in Ancient Rome?

6. What sports did they do in Ancient Rome?

7. What is Fez?

8. What is special about the University of Karueein?

9. Which country had the first university in Europe?

10. Where is Oxford University?

11. What subjects were taught in universities in Europe?

12. What is the oldest university in the United States?

13. What are the two oldest universities in Canada?

14. Name some subjects that were taught in universities in Canada.

First Schools in Canada

Listening Activity 2

Exercise 1: Get Ready to Listen

□ □ **A.** Work with a partner. Look at the picture of a school in Canada from long ago.

1. Give two ways that you think the school was different from schools today.

2. Give two ways that you think the school was the same as schools today.

Did You Know?	The university that has the most students in the world is the State University of New York. It has more than 150 000 students.

B. Read these questions aloud with a partner. What do you think the story will be about?

1. Two hundred years ago in North America:
   a) everyone went to school
   b) most children went to school
   c) most children were educated at home

2. Canada's first schools were:
   a) big
   b) small

3. The buildings were made of:
   a) stone
   b) wood
   c) mud

4. Students from different grades had:
   a) one teacher
   b) many teachers

5. The teachers cut wood:
   a) to make books
   b) to make desks
   c) to keep the classroom warm

6. The children used water:
   a) to drink
   b) to wash the blackboards
   c) to wash the desks

7. The teachers counted:
   a) the students
   b) the books
   c) the days

8. The teachers rang the bell:
   a) at lunchtime
   b) on Saturday
   c) in the morning and afternoon

9. Which students went to high school?
   a) all the students
   b) students who wanted to be teachers
   c) students who wanted to be farmers

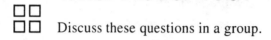 **Exercise 2: Listen for Meaning**

Listen to the story. What is the story about?

Exercise 3: Listen for Details

Go back to the questions. While you listen, choose the correct answers.

What About You?

 Discuss these questions in a group.

1. What subjects did you study in elementary school?
2. What subjects do people study in high school?
3. For how many years did you go to elementary school?
4. What did you like about elementary school?
5. What did you not like about elementary school?

My School

Write about a school you attended in the past.

Clothing

Who Wears What?

Work with the partner. Choose the correct answers.

1. What does a man wear to work?
   a) a suit
   b) shorts
   c) pyjamas

2. What does a person wear in the rain?
   a) a nightgown
   b) sandals
   c) a raincoat

3. What does a nurse wear to work?
   a) a uniform
   b) blue jeans
   c) a sweater

4. Who wears a bikini?
   a) an old man
   b) a young woman
   c) a police officer

5. What does a person wear outside in cold weather?
   a) a coat
   b) a blouse
   c) a T-shirt

6. What do people wear to the beach?
   a) sun-hats
   b) wool hats
   c) gloves

7. What does a bride usually wear in North America?
   a) a white dress
   b) shorts
   c) sneakers

8. What does a dancer wear?
   a) a leotard
   b) skates
   c) wool gloves

9. What does a football player wear?
   a) a helmet
   b) loafers
   c) a necklace

10. What does a fisherman wear?
    a) high boots
    b) earrings
    c) a fur hat

11. What does a child wear outside in cold weather?
    a) a bathing suit
    b) a snowsuit
    c) short socks

12. Who wears a diaper?
    a) a baby
    b) a firefighter
    c) a turtle

The Price is Right

Partner A

Yoshimi and Aki went shopping. Your partner has a list of the prices Aki paid for his clothes. Copy the chart. Write the price your partner tells you.

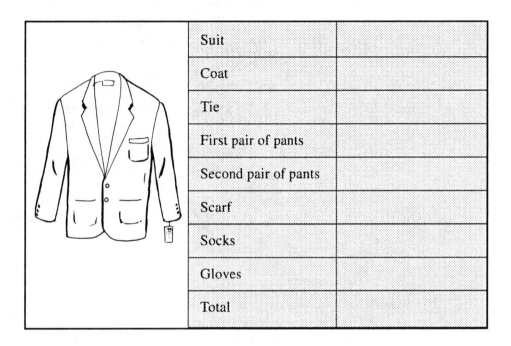

Suit	
Coat	
Tie	
First pair of pants	
Second pair of pants	
Scarf	
Socks	
Gloves	
Total	

Here are the prices of Yoshimi's clothes. Read the prices to your partner. Your partner will write them down.

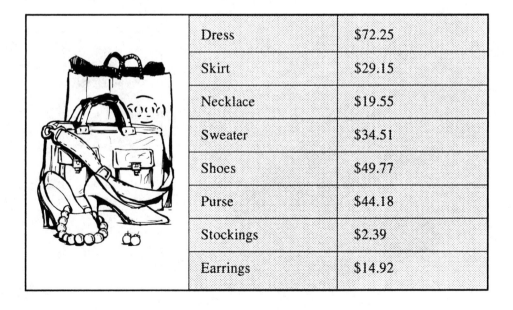

Dress	$72.25
Skirt	$29.15
Necklace	$19.55
Sweater	$34.51
Shoes	$49.77
Purse	$44.18
Stockings	$2.39
Earrings	$14.92

Who spent more money, Yoshimi or Aki?

Partner B

Yoshimi and Aki went shopping. Below is a list of the prices Aki paid for his new clothes. Read the prices to your partner. Your partner will write them down.

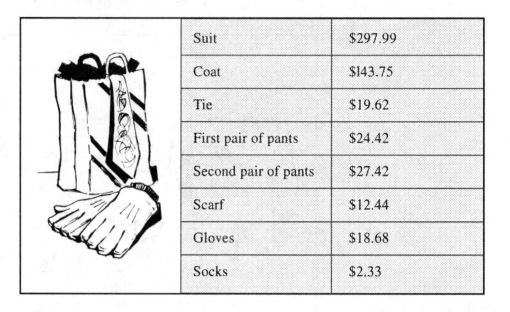

Suit	$297.99
Coat	$143.75
Tie	$19.62
First pair of pants	$24.42
Second pair of pants	$27.42
Scarf	$12.44
Gloves	$18.68
Socks	$2.33

Now ask your partner what Yoshimi paid for each item. Copy the chart. Write the prices your partner tells you.

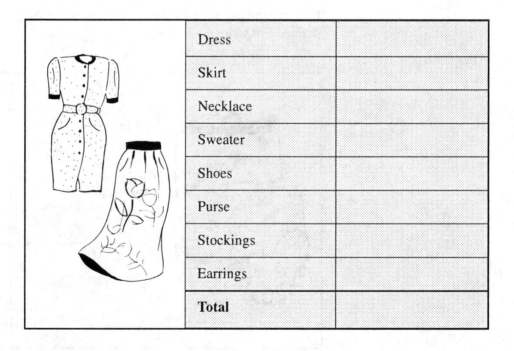

Dress	
Skirt	
Necklace	
Sweater	
Shoes	
Purse	
Stockings	
Earrings	
Total	

Who spent more money, Yoshimi or Aki?

Match the Opposites

Find the opposites. Write the answer beside the number.

1.	white	tight
2.	low	black
3.	loose	short
4.	long	light
5.	small	high
6.	hard	wide
7.	ugly	big
8.	uncomfortable	under
9.	dark	soft
10.	narrow	top
11.	over	beautiful
12.	bottom	plain
13.	fancy	comfortable
14.	old	new

How to Buy a Winter Coat

> **Listening Activity 3**

Exercise 1: Get Ready to Listen

☐ ☐ **A.** Work with a partner. Look at the pictures. How many parts of the coat and jacket can you name?

**coat   jacket   sleeves   collar   zipper
pockets   buttons   label   pricetag**

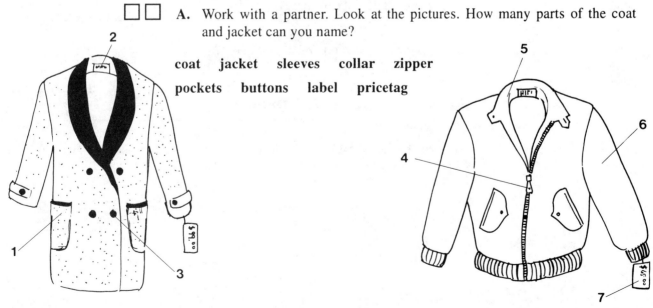

☐☐ **B.** Read the questions aloud with a partner. What do you think the information will be about?

1. Jackets are:

   a) hard to find

   b) short

   c) long

2. The length of a coat is:

   a) to the hips

   b) to the waist

   c) to the knees

3. What are many winter coats made of?

   a) silk

   b) wool

   c) cotton

4. Some jackets and coats are filled with:

   a) feathers

   b) cotton

   c) flowers

5. The label inside the coat tells you:

   a) how much the coat costs

   b) how warm the coat will be

   c) the colour of the coat

6. What should you check to see if the coat fits?

   a) the price

   b) the length of the sleeves

   c) the buttons or zipper

7. What should you check to see if you like the coat?

   a) the style

   b) the price

   c) the label

○○ Exercise 2: Listen for Meaning

Listen to the information. What is it about?

○○ Exercise 3: Listen for Details

Go back to the questions. While you listen, choose the correct answers. For some questions, you can choose more than one answer.

Too Many Zippers

Choose the correct word for each space.

zipper   jacket   arms   pockets   designer   money

There is a clothing designer in California who
loves _____. He also loves zippers. So he
      1
designed a special jacket for himself. It has
70 pockets. Each pocket has a _____.
          2

Some pockets are inside
the _____, and some
3
pockets are outside. Some pockets are on the back of the jacket and some
pockets are even under the _____. Once this _____ spent 27 minutes
        4   **5**
looking in his pockets. He couldn't remember where he had put his _____.
                                                              6

Money and Banking

Canadian Money
Interaction
Cultural Information

What About You?
Interaction

Writing a Cheque
Writing
Interaction

Banks
Reading

The Loonie
Vocabulary

At the Bank
Listening Activity 4

Saying Amounts of Money
Pronunciation

Making Change
Interaction

Money Matters
Crossword Puzzle

Canadian Money

In Canada we use two kinds of money: coins and bills. Coins are made of metal. Each coin has a picture on it. Each coin is worth a different amount of money. Bills are made of paper. Each bill is a different colour. Each bill is worth a different amount of money.

☐☐ 1. Work with a partner. Look at the pictures of the Canadian coins. Make a chart similar to the one below. Write the name, the value and the metal, and say what the picture shows.

What coin is called					
Value of coin					
What coin is made of					
Picture on coin					

What picture is on the back of each coin?

2. Do you know which bills we have in Canada? Work with a partner. Choose from the list.

$1	$50
$2	$100
$5	$200
$10	$500
$20	$1000
$25	

3. What colours are the different bills? Choose the colour for each bill we have in Canada.

purple   **blue**   **pink**   **orange**   **orange/brown**   **green**   **gold**

4. What pictures are on the bills?

What About You?

Find out if there are students who have money from other countries. Ask them about the money they have.

1. How many different coins do they have?
2. How many different bills do they have?
3. What is the value of their money, compared with Canadian money?

Write the information in a chart similar to the one below.

Students' Countries			
Coins			
Bills			
Values			

Did You Know?	Today, the Hudson's Bay Company is a department store called "the Bay." In the early days in Canada, the Hudson's Bay Company was so important that it printed its own money.

Writing a Cheque

Exercise 1: Get Ready

☐☐ Work with a partner. Look at the blank cheque below. Copy the cheque. Then make out the cheque (write in the information) to Bell Canada, for $43.74. It is due on February 17th.

```
                                                    _____19___

Pay to the
order of  _____  $_____

Sum of  _____ /100 Dollars

                                         _____
```

Exercise 2: Exchange Information

Partner A

Cover Partner B's section. Give your partner these instructions. He or she will write the cheques. Then follow the instructions your partner gives you.

1. Write a cheque to pay your rent. Make it out to Mr. Smith, for $325.00. It is due on January 1st.

2. Write a cheque to pay your MasterCard bill. The amount is $187.33. It is for November 26th.

3. Make out a cheque to pay your bill at the Bay. It is for $73.46. The date is September 16th.

4. You owe your friend $21.69. Write a cheque to her. Date it August 14th.

Partner B

Cover Partner A's section. Write the cheques your partner describes. Then give your partner these instructions.

1. Write a cheque to pay your bill at Eaton's. It is for $35.99. It is due April 3rd.

2. You owe your brother $16.86. Pay him on May 12th.

3. You have to pay your Visa bill. Make out a cheque for $138.98. It is due on October 29th.

4. You must pay your income tax. Write a cheque to the Receiver General of Canada (the Government of Canada) for $256.88. It must be paid by April 30th.

Banks

Exercise 1: Read Quickly for General Ideas

Banks

Where do you put your money to keep it safe? Do you put it in a jar? Do you put it under your bed? Perhaps you put it in a box in your cupboard. Some people even keep cash in the refrigerator. They think no one will find it there.

If you want to keep your money safe, a bank is a good place to put it. There are other reasons to put your money in the bank. At a bank you can borrow money, or you can get more money by earning interest.

People have put money in banks for thousands of years. The ancient Greeks put their money in jars. In Babylon, over 5000 years ago, people kept their money in temples. The ancient Chinese and the Romans also had banking systems. In the fifteenth and sixteenth centuries in Europe, many people were bankers. Anyone who had a safe box, and wanted to trade coins, was called a banker.

One of the first banks, which we still use today, is the piggy bank. The piggy bank started in England 1000 years ago. At this time, people did not have much metal to make things for the house. Instead, they used a kind of orange clay, called pygg. They used this clay to make dishes, cups, pots and jars. People often saved their money in clay pots and jars. One day a potter decided to make the pot look like its name. He shaped it to look like a pig. Today many people have small banks at home to keep coins. Even if they don't look like pigs, they are called piggy banks.

Exercise 2: Read Carefully for Details

Work with a partner. Look in the text for the answers.

1. Name three places people sometimes keep their money.

2. Give three reasons people put money in banks.

3. People have put money in banks for hundreds of years. **T** (true) or **F** (false)?

4. Where did the ancient Greeks put their money?

5. The Romans and the Chinese had banking systems. **T F**

6. In Europe, many people were called bankers. **T F**

7. The piggy bank started in France.   **T F**

8. How did people make things such as dishes and cups?

9. Where did people save their money?

10. What did a potter decide to do one day?

11. Today, what do people call small banks at home?

The Loonie

Choose the correct word for each space.

eyes   dollar   laugh   picture   bird

The Canadian _____ coin is called a loonie. It is called a loonie because it

        1

has a _____ of a loon on it. A loon is a strange _____ that lives in

     2   **3**

Canada. The loon has bright red _____, a funny walk and a strange

                                    4

_____. The word "loony" sometimes means "crazy."

5

At the Bank

> **Listening Activity 4**

Exercise 1: Get Ready to Listen

☐☐ Read these questions aloud with a partner. What do you think the conversation will be about?

1. The man wants to:

   a) deposit money

   b) cash a cheque

   c) open a bank account

2. The cheque is for:

   a) $105.33

   b) $115.33

   c) $150.33

3. Mr. Williams has to:

   a) sign the cheque

   b) read the cheque

   c) return the cheque

4. In his change he needs:

   a) a quarter

   b) a dime

   c) a penny

○○ **Exercise 2: Listen for Meaning**

Before you begin, cover Exercise 4.

Listen to the conversation. What is the conversation about?

○○ **Exercise 3: Listen for Details**

Go back to the questions. While you listen, choose the correct answers.

○○ **Exercise 4: Listen for Sounds**

While you listen, write the missing words.

At the Bank

Teller:	Yes, sir. Can I help you?
Mr. Williams:	Yes. I'_____ like to cash this cheque.
Teller:	OK. Let's see. The cheque is for $150.33. Do you want that _____ big bills ?
Mr. Williams:	Big bills?
Teller:	Yes. _____ you want that in fifties?
Mr. Williams:	No. I prefer smaller bills.
Teller:	OK. How about six twenties _____ three tens?
Mr. Williams:	That's fine.
Teller:	Please sign the back _____ the cheque. We need your signature on the back.
Mr. Williams:	Sure. No problem.
Teller:	OK. Here'_____ your money. Six twenties and three tens. That makes $150. And here's your change. Three dimes and three pennies.
Mr. Williams:	Oh. I need a quarter for _____ parking meter. Can I please have a quarter, a nickel and three pennies?
Teller:	Sure. Here _____ are. A quarter, a nickel and three cents. Anything else I can do for you?
Mr. Williams:	No. I guess that'_____ it for today. Thanks.
Teller:	You're welcome. Have _____ nice day.

Exercise 5: Practise Speaking

☐☐   Practise reading the dialogue with a partner. Then change roles and read it again.

Saying Amounts of Money

We say $43.76 like this:

> forty-three dollars and seventy-six cents
>
> OR
>
> forty-three seventy six

Work with a partner. Write two ways to say each of these amounts:

> $61.22
>
> $57.17
>
> $39.09
>
> $88.68
>
> $43.92
>
> $21.54

Making Change

1. For $20.00, we can use a twenty-dollar bill, two ten-dollar bills, four five-dollar bills, etc. Write two combinations of bills you can use to make these amounts of money.

    > $22
    >
    > $56
    >
    > $49
    >
    > $86
    >
    > $32
    >
    > $51

2. For 75 cents, we can use three quarters, seven dimes and a nickel, etc. Write two different combinations of coins you can use to make these amounts of money.

    > 61 cents
    >
    > 39 cents
    >
    > 46 cents
    >
    > 78 cents
    >
    > 21 cents
    >
    > 8 cents

Money Matters

Crossword Puzzle

Across

2. When you buy something, you can pay by cheque or you can use _____.

3. To keep your money safe, put it in the _____.

4. A 25-cent coin is called a _____.

8. A ten-cent coin is called a _____.

9. Dimes, nickels, pennies and quarters are _____.

11. Coins are made of _____.

12. A one-cent coin is called a _____.

Down

1. Bills are made of _____.

2. You can write a _____ to pay a bill.

5. You can put your money in a savings or a chequing _____ at the bank.

6. The colour of a five-dollar bill is _____.

7. In Canada there are two kinds of money: coins and _____.

10. Put your money in the bank to keep it _____.

Unit 6

Jobs People Have

White Collar, Blue Collar
  Reading
  Cultural Information

Working Outside
  Vocabulary
  Writing

Who Earns Most?
  Interaction

Saying Numbers
  Interaction
  Pronunciation

White Collar, Blue Collar

Exercise 1: Get Ready to Read

☐☐ Work with a partner. Look at the pictures.

1. Name the jobs that you see.
2. What kinds of clothes do people wear to do their jobs?

📖 Exercise 2: Read Quickly for General Ideas

White Collar, Blue Collar

People do many different kinds of jobs. Sometimes we can tell the kind of work that people do by the kind of clothing that they wear. For example, you do not know that a person is a police officer if he or she does not wear a uniform. There are other people who wear special clothes for their work. Soldiers, ballet dancers, religious leaders and people who do sports have special clothes that they wear for work.

When people work in offices and banks, they wear clothes such as dresses or suits. People who are secretaries, bank tellers and managers, or work in other office jobs, are called white-collar workers. This name comes from the collars of the shirts that employees wore to do inside work in the past. The shirts were white; the collars were white.

In service industries, many people wear uniforms. For example, porters, waiters, police officers and bus drivers wear uniforms. Mechanics, letter carriers, plumbers and elevator operators are also uniformed workers. Many people who do outside or manual jobs wear uniforms. These people are called blue-collar workers. This name comes from the blue shirts some workers wore with their uniforms in the past. The shirts were blue; the collars were blue.

📖 Exercise 3: Read Carefully for Details

Work with a partner. Look in the text for the answers.

1. How can we tell the kind of work people do?
2. Give some examples of people who wear special clothes for their work.
3. What do people in offices or banks usually wear to work?
4. What does the name "white collar" come from?
5. Is "white collar" a good description of what people wear today?
6. Give two examples of jobs in service industries.
7. What do letter carriers and mechanics both wear?
8. Which people are called blue-collar workers?
9. Give two examples of blue-collar workers.

Exercise 4: Review Vocabulary

Identify which of these jobs are white-collar and which are blue-collar.

secretary	carpenter
bank teller	elevator operator
bus driver	mechanic
waiter	manager
porter	plumber

Working Outside

Exercise 1: Get Ready

☐☐ Many people work outside. There are many different jobs to do. Look at the picture of people working outside. Find the people with the jobs below.

**telephone mechanic   police officer   letter carrier   bus driver   porter
garbage collector   firefighter   window washer   mover   street musician**

Exercise 2: Practise Writing

Use these verbs to write ten sentences. Describe what the people in the drawing are doing.

wash   carry   fix   deliver   ask   open   drive   collect   stop

clean   save

Who Earns Most?

Exercise 1: Get Ready

A. Work in a group. Look at the pictures.

1. Name the jobs you see.

2. What do you think is the salary for each job?

B. Cover the information in Exercise 2. Look at the sentences below. Predict **T** (true) or **F** (false).

1. A taxi driver earns more than a cook.

2. A construction worker earns more than a sales clerk.

3. A secretary earns more than a mechanic.

4. A hairdresser makes less than a sales clerk.

5. A bank teller and a secretary make the same amount of money.

6. A mechanic and a taxi driver make the same amount of money.

7. A mechanic makes more than a sales clerk.

8. A sales clerk makes more than a bank teller.

Exercise 2: Transfer Information

Look at the chart of weekly salaries. Then check the answers that you predicted.

taxi driver	$300
sales clerk	$200
mechanic	$325
secretary	$345
bank teller	$360
construction worker	$440
cook	$280
hairdresser	$300

Saying Numbers

We can say numbers such as 462 like this:

four hundred and sixty-two
OR
four sixty-two

Did You Know?   The numbers we use are called Arabic numbers. We sometimes use Roman numerals. I, II, III, IV, V are examples of Roman numerals.

Partner A

Cover your partner's numbers. Read five numbers from your list to your partner. Then write five numbers that your partner says. Then repeat.

953

417

211

629

840

(Stop)

329

708

862

392

846

Partner B

Cover your partner's numbers. Write the numbers your partner reads to you. Then read five numbers from your list to your partner. Then repeat.

129

522

311

456

902

(Stop)

670

485

772

156

872

Unit 7

Food

International Foods

Exercise 1: Get Ready to Discuss

Work in a group. Look at the pictures of food from different countries. How many can you name?

Match each food to a country.

1.	shish kebab	Japan
2.	egg rolls	Malaysia
3.	borscht	Italy
4.	sushi	Mexico
5.	Yorkshire pudding	China
6.	Wiener schnitzel	England
7.	satay	Russia
8.	lasagna	Iran
9.	croissants	Germany
10.	tacos	France

shish kebab   egg rolls   borscht

Yorkshire pudding   satay

sushi   Wiener schnitzel

lasagna   croissants   tacos

Exercise 2: Express Yourself

Discuss these questions in a group.

1. What kinds of food do you like to eat?
2. Name three foods that you like to eat in your home.
3. Name three foods that you like to eat in Canada.
4. Do you eat any new foods in Canada? What are they?

Exercise 3: Practise Grammar

Write three questions to ask another student about food that he or she likes to eat.

Bread

Exercise 1: Get Ready to Read

Work in a group. Look at the picture.

1. Name some kinds of bread.
2. Name some things you can put on bread.
3. Name some things bread is made from.

Exercise 2: Read Carefully for Information

Work with a partner. Look in the text for the answers.

Bread

Bread is a basic food in Canada. Many Canadians eat bread two or three times a day. They have toast for breakfast. They have a sandwich for lunch. Then they have bread and butter with their supper.

Most of the bread we eat in Canada is made from wheat. Wheat is a grain that grows in western Canada. The wheat is made into flour. Then it is mixed with milk, eggs and other ingredients to make bread. Different countries use other grains to make bread. For example, in Mexico, corn is used to make some kinds of bread. Oats and rye are other grains that can be used to make bread.

In stores, you can buy many different kinds of bread that are made from wheat. White sliced bread is good for toast or sandwiches. Rolls are good to eat with lunch. Bagels are popular in some places. A bagel is a round roll with a hole in the centre. French bread is a long bread that is soft in the middle and crusty on the outside. Restaurants often serve French bread.

You can find many other kinds of bread in Canada that are made from different kinds of flour. Some examples of breads made from different kinds of flour are rye, corn, pumpernickel, whole wheat, Italian and pita bread.

People like to put different things on bread. You can spread butter or margarine on bread. You can put jam or peanut butter on bread too, and you can put cream cheese on a bagel. You don't have to put anything on bread, though. It's delicious by itself, especially when it is hot and fresh.

1. How often do Canadians eat bread?

2. How do Canadians like to eat bread for:

    a) breakfast?

    b) lunch?

    c) supper?

3. What is wheat?

4. What are some ingredients used to make bread?

5. Name some other grains that are used to make bread.

6. What is white sliced bread used for?

7. Where is French bread served?

8. Name some other kinds of breads.

9. Name some things you can put on bread or bagels.

10. What kind of bread do you like to eat?

44

Exercise 3: Review Vocabulary

Read the text again. Find the word that means the opposite.

bad

short

hard

inside

same

cold

stale

How We Make Bread

Exercise 1: Read Carefully for Information

Work with a partner. Look at the pictures. Read the text. Then use the information to write a sentence for each picture.

How We Make Bread

We make bread at a bakery. Bread is made from flour, eggs, milk and several other things. The ingredients are mixed to make dough. Then we make the dough into loaves. The loaves of bread are baked in the oven. After this, the bread is cut and put into bags. Then it goes to the store so people can buy it.

Exercise 2: Tell the Story

Tell your partner how bread is made. Use your own words. Use the pictures to help you. Then your partner will tell you how bread is made.

Coffee or Tea

Exercise 1: Read Quickly for General Ideas

Coffee or Tea

Coffee and tea are the most popular drinks in the world. Coffee is a favourite drink of Canadians. Many Canadians like to start their day with a cup of coffee. At work, they may take a coffee break. A coffee break is a time to stop and relax for a few minutes over a cup of coffee or a snack.

Why is coffee so popular? For one thing, it has a rich, strong taste that many people like. It is served hot, with milk, cream or sugar. Many people like coffee in the morning because it helps them wake up. Coffee has caffeine in it. Caffeine gives people more energy.

Every day, millions of people all over the world drink tea. Tea is the national drink of China, Japan, England and Russia. In England, it is a custom to drink tea in the afternoon. In Japan, drinking tea is a social custom and there are special rules for tea drinking.

Tea comes from tea leaves. We make tea by pouring boiling water on dried tea leaves. People usually drink hot tea, but it can be served cold. Some people like to drink tea with milk or cream. Other people hate milk or cream in tea, but they put in honey, sugar or lemon. Tea also has some caffeine in it.

Exercise 2: Read Carefully for Details

Work with a partner. Look in the text for the answers.

1. What are the most popular drinks in the world?

2. What drink do Canadians like best?

3. A coffee break is a time to start work.   **T** (true) or **F** (false)?

4. Name three things people like to put in coffee.

5. What does caffeine do?

6. Name three countries where people like to drink tea.

7. People in England like to drink tea in the morning.   **T   F**

8. How do we make tea?

9. Name five things people put in tea.

The Story of Tea

Listening Activity 5

Exercise 1: Get Ready to Listen

Look at the pictures. Then read the questions aloud with a partner. What do you think the story will be about?

1. Where did the first story happen?

    a) in England

    b) in the Far East

    c) in India

2. What did the religious man do every day?

    a) eat

    b) pray

    c) fall asleep

3. He did not sleep for:

    a) three years

    b) five years

    c) seven years

4. What did he eat?

    a) his dinner

    b) some leaves

    c) some flowers

5. What happened after he ate the tea leaves?

    a) he felt good

    b) he fell asleep

    c) he had dinner

6. When did tea come to England?

    a) in the 1600s

    b) in the 1700s

    c) in the 1800s

7. Where did the woman get the tea leaves?

    a) from the store

    b) from the cupboard

    c) from the Orient

8. Who did she invite over to her house?

    a) her mother

    b) her friends

    c) her neighbour

48

Exercise 2: Listen for Meaning

Listen to the story on the tape. What is the story about?

Exercise 3: Listen for Details

Go back to the questions. While you listen, choose the correct answers.

The Story of Coffee

Exercise 1: Get Ready to Read

What do you know about the discovery of coffee? Work with a partner. Choose the best answers. Use the pictures to help you.

1. Coffee was first discovered in:

   a) Ethiopia

   b) Brazil

   c) China

2. The animal that first ate coffee beans was:

   a) a fish

   b) a goat

   c) an elephant

3. The animal that ate the coffee beans became:

   a) sleepy

   b) bored

   c) excited

4. Before people add water to coffee beans they:

   a) eat the coffee beans

   b) smell the coffee beans

   c) grind the coffee beans

Exercise 2: Read Quickly for General Ideas

The Story of Coffee

Coffee comes from the seeds of a coffee plant. These seeds are called beans. The coffee beans are roasted to make coffee. Coffee plants grow in hot places. They need a lot of sun and a lot of rain.

The story of coffee is very interesting. It started about 850 years ago, in Ethiopia. According to the story, a goatherd named Kaldi once saw his goats eat the berries of a plant. When the goats ate the berries, they jumped around and acted very strangely. Kaldi tasted the berries. He thought they were very good. He talked to his friends about this new food.

For a long time, people did not drink coffee. They ate it! They crushed the berries and rolled them into a ball. They ate the ball of crushed berries when they travelled. Some people even used the leaves from the coffee plant to make wine.

Later, people started to find new ways to use coffee. They ground and roasted the beans. Then they put the beans in hot water to make a hot drink. The drink became popular in Egypt and Turkey. Later, it became popular in Europe too.

Each country has its own way of drinking coffee. In North America, people add cream and sugar. The French put hot milk in their coffee. Italians like to put cinnamon or chocolate in their coffee. In the Middle East, people drink strong black coffee. Irish coffee is the strongest coffee. It has whisky in it.

Exercise 3: Read Carefully for Details

Work with a partner. Look in the text for the answers.

1. Where do coffee plants grow?

2. What do they need to grow well?

3. When did the story of coffee start? Where?

4. What did the goats eat?

5. What did the goats do?

6. How did people eat coffee berries?

7. When did they eat them?

8. How did people use coffee beans later?

9. Where did the drink become popular?

10. How do people drink coffee in these places?

    a) North America   d) the Middle East

    b) France   e) Ireland

    c) Italy

Exercise 4: Tell the Story

Tell the story of coffee to your partner. Use your own words. Then your partner will tell you the story.

The World's Strongest Coffee

Brazil grows a lot of coffee. Some of the coffee is very strong. One kind of coffee from Brazil is so strong that if you drink it, you will stay awake for 24 hours. If you put in milk or cream, the coffee will not be so strong. Then you will stay awake only 18 hours.

A Cup of Coffee

Listen for Sounds

Write the expressions your teacher dictates.

The Honey Hunters

Exercise 1: Get Ready to Read

Work in a group. Discuss these questions.

1. Where is Nepal?

2. Is Nepal a rich country?

3. How do people earn a living in Nepal?

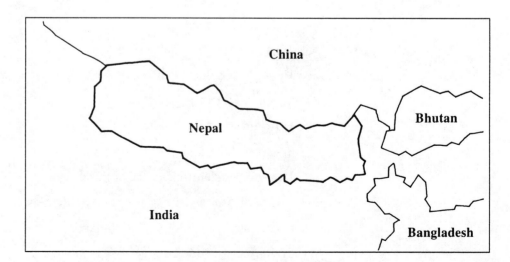

📖 Exercise 2: Read Quickly for General Ideas

The Honey Hunters

In one village in central Nepal, people have a hard life. Food is not easy to grow and it is not easy to find. People are farmers but the land is not rich. Sometimes people go to the forest to find more food. Men hunt for animals. Once a year they also look for something special. They look for honey.

The honey hunt is not for everyone. Only nine men from one family go on the hunt for honey. They hunt for three weeks at a time. They hunt in the spring and in the fall.

The leader of the honey hunt is a man called Mani Lal. He is 64 years old. How does Mani Lal hunt? He leads his men into the forest. The strongest man carries a ladder. The ladder is made of rope but it is very long and very heavy.

Mani Lal uses the ladder to go down a big cliff near the bees' nest. When he is near the nest, the bees get angry. They leave the nest and attack Mani Lal. He is not afraid because the hunters make a fire, with smoke. The bees are afraid of the smoke and fly away.

Mani Lal works hard taking the nests to get the honey. The other hunters help Mani Lal send down the honey in a basket.

Every year hunters take 80 nests. They share the honey and Mani Lal sells the wax from the bees' nest. He sells the wax for $7 for 2.5 kilograms. In a poor country such as Nepal, this is good money. Mani Lal and the hunters are happy with the honey and the money from the wax.

Mani Lal is an old man. He has no sons to continue after him. When Mani Lal dies, maybe the honey hunt in central Nepal will stop.

Exercise 3: Read Carefully for Details

Work with a partner. Look in the text for the answers.

1. Why is life hard in Nepal?

2. How often do men hunt for honey?

3. Give the rules of the honey hunt.

    a) Who goes on the hunt?

    b) How long does it last?

    c) When does it take place?

4. Who leads the honey hunters?

5. Why does the strongest man carry the ladder?

6. Where are the bees' nests?

7. When do the bees become angry?

8. Why isn't Mani Lal afraid of the bees?

9. How do the other hunters help Mani Lal?

10. How many nests do the hunters take?

11. What do they do with the honey?

12. What does Mani Lal sell?

13. How much do people pay for the wax?

14. The hunters are sad at the end of the hunt.   **T** (true) or **F** (false)?

15. Mani Lal's son will continue to hunt honey.   **T   F**

16. What may happen when Mani Lal dies?

Ice Cream

Exercise 1: Get Ready to Read

Work in a group. Discuss these questions.

1. Can you name some popular flavours of ice cream?

2. Where can you buy ice cream in Canada?

3. Where can you buy ice cream in other countries?

4. Which country do you think invented ice cream?

Exercise 2: Read Quickly for General Ideas

Ice Cream

Ice cream is a very popular dessert in Canada. Children and adults like the cold, sweet taste of ice cream. But this popular dessert doesn't come from Canada. It doesn't come from a cold country. It comes from China.

Ice cream began in China 4000 years ago. That was the first time that people had cows for milk, and milk was a special treat. The rulers of China had a favourite food. They ate this food as a dessert. It was a dish of rice cooked with milk and spices. The rice and milk dish was put in snow to make it cold. Later, the Chinese began to mix fruit juice with the milk and rice. They sold these ice milks and ice fruits on the street, as desserts.

Next, people in Italy began to make ice milk and fruit ice. They had a special recipe for their desserts. The desserts took a long time to make, and only rich people ate the ice desserts.

Soon the French started to make frozen desserts. They added flavours such as lemon, lime, cherry and strawberry. They also added cream to the ice desserts. This made the desserts more like our modern ice cream.

Then the Italians learned that if they added salt to snow and ice, they had ice cream that was more solid. They sold their ice cream in the streets. Italian ice cream is popular in Canada today.

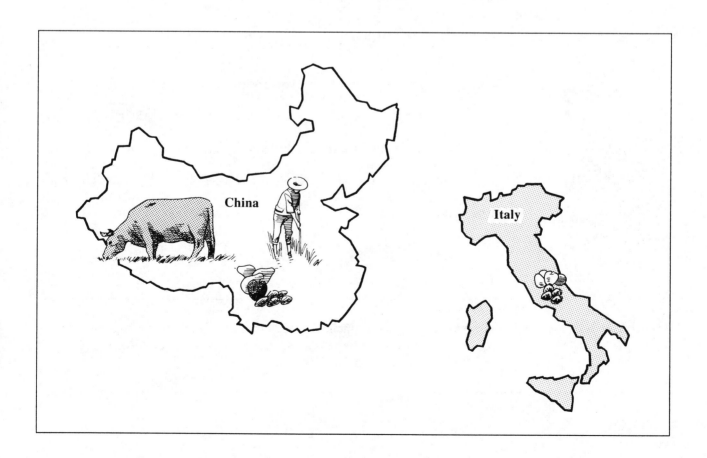

Exercise 3: Read Carefully for Details

Work with a partner. Look in the text for the answers.

1. Why do people like ice cream?
2. Where does ice cream come from?
3. Why was milk a special treat in China?
4. How did the Chinese make their special desserts at first?
5. What did they add later?
6. Who ate ice cream in Italy?
7. Name some flavours the French added to their frozen dessert.
8. What did the French add to their dessert to make it like modern ice cream?
9. Why did the Italians add salt to their ice cream?
10. Where did the Italians sell ice cream?

The Worst Flavour

Choose the correct word for each space.

flavour   shops   people   money   salmon   vanilla

Some ice cream _____ sell many flavours of ice cream. Chocolate and _____
               1   2
are the most popular. But one ice cream shop has a special flavour: chocolate

_____ surprise. It tastes terrible! But the _____ is very unusual, so many
3   4
_____ want to try it. The ice cream shop makes a lot of _____ from chocolate
5   6
salmon surprise.

| **Did You Know?** | Many people bring their lunches to work or class. They often bring their lunches in a brown paper bag. That is why taking your lunch to work or class is called "brown bagging." |

Miss Vickie's Potato Chips

Exercise 1: Get Ready to Listen

☐☐ **A.** Work with a partner. Read this paragraph quickly. Then make a chart similar to the one that follows the paragraph. Fill in the chart with information from the text.

Miss Vickie's Potato Chips

Most potato chips are fried in lots of oil. They taste greasy. They also have lots of salt, and other things are added to keep them fresh. Miss Vickie's Potato Chips are cooked in peanut oil. They have only a little sea salt. Nothing else is on the potatoes. They are very fresh, and they taste delicious.

	Most potato chips	Miss Vickie's Potato Chips
Method of cooking		
Salt		
Other things added		
Taste		

☐☐ **B.** Read these sentences aloud with a partner. What do you think the story will be about?

1. Potatoes are healthy because they have vitamin C.

2. Vickie Kerr lives on a potato farm with her husband and two children.

3. Vickie wanted to make potato chips that tasted fresh.

4. Vickie bought potatoes to make potato chips.

5. Vickie has a company that makes potato chips.

6. At first, Vickie and her neighbours made potato chips in her kitchen.

7. Vickie and her neighbours cut and fried the potatoes in the afternoon.

8. Vickie took the chips to the stores by car.

9. It takes fourteen minutes to make potato chips.

10. One place that you can buy Miss Vickie's Potato Chips is the Yukon.

☐☐ Exercise 2: Listen for Meaning

Listen to the story. What is the story about?

☐☐ Exercise 3: Listen for Details

Go back to the sentences. While you listen, write **T** (true) or **F** (false).

Exercise 4: Tell the Story

☐☐ Tell the story of Miss Vickie's Potato Chips to your partner. Use your own words. Then your partner will tell you the story.

Exercise 5: Practise Spelling

Write these words. Fill in the missing letters.

potat–

ch–ps

s–lt

o–l

ic– c–eam

ch–col–te

v–nill–

ch–rry

sa–mon

Travel and Transportation

City Traffic

Exercise 1: Get Ready to Read

Discuss these questions in a group.

1. Do cars obey traffic lights here?

2. Do people obey traffic lights here?

3. Are there traffic lights in other cities that you know?

4. Where do people obey traffic lights better, here or in other cities that you know?

Exercise 2: Read Quickly for General Ideas

City Traffic

When people began to drive cars in the city, the cars did not go very fast. At least, we don't think they were very fast compared with cars today. The cars went about 25 kilometres per hour. At that time, people thought this was a fast way to move, so in Britain they passed a law. When someone wanted to drive a car on a city street, another person had to walk ahead, waving a red flag. This was to warn people that a dangerous vehicle was approaching.

Soon, more people began to drive cars in the city. The cars started to move faster. People who lived in the city needed a way to stop the cars so that they could cross the street.

The first traffic light was in London, England in 1868. It worked by gas. It seemed to work well. Then one day something happened with the gas and the traffic light exploded. The explosion killed a police officer. After that, people didn't use traffic lights for another 50 years. They thought they were dangerous.

Today, traffic lights are safe. They work by electricity. In all the big cities and in small towns in Canada, there are traffic lights. When people want to cross the street, they look at the colour of the light. A red light means "Stop." A green light means "Go." A yellow light means "Wait." When the light is yellow, it will soon turn red.

You can cross the street when the light is green. But you still have to be careful. In some cities, cars can turn right when the light is red. So before you cross the street, look to the left and look to the right. Then stay in the crosswalk and you will be safe.

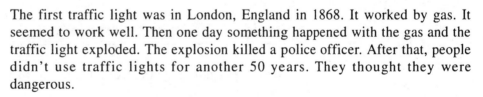

Exercise 3: Read Carefully for Details

Work with a partner. Look in the text for the answers.

1. When people began to drive cars in the city, how fast were the cars?

2. How did people in the city know that a car was coming?

3. When cars went faster, why did people need to find a new way to stop the cars?

4. Where was the first traffic light?

5. How did the first traffic light work? What happened to it?

6. What happened to the police officer?

7. When did people begin to use traffic lights again?

8. How do traffic lights work today?

9. All traffic lights are in big cities. True or false?

10. What do the colours mean?

    a) green

    b) yellow

    c) red

11. What happens after the light turns yellow?

12. When the light turns green, what do you do?

13. Why do you have to be careful in some Canadian cities?

14. Where is the right place to stay when you are crossing the street?

Exercise 4: Review Vocabulary

Read the text again. Find the word that means the opposite.

1. dangerous
2. small
3. stop
4. left

5. after
6. slow
7. behind
8. start

Did You Know?   Transportation in the city can be difficult when there are many cars on the road. It is even more difficult in winter, when there is ice and snow on the ground. Canadians have learned to cope with bad weather conditions. Streets are cleaned very quickly after a snow storm in Canadian cities. Most of the time, people go to work or school with few problems.

Travel to Cities in Canada

Partner A

Look at the map of Canadian cities labelled **Map A.** It shows the distances between some cities. Ask your partner for the information that you are missing. Write the information on your copy of the map.

Example:

Question: What is the distance between Winnipeg and Toronto?

Answer: 2099 kilometres.

Then give your partner the information he or she needs.

Map A

Partner B

Look at the map of Canadian cities labelled **Map B.** It shows the distances between some cities. Give your partner the information that he or she needs. Then ask your partner for the information that you are missing. Write the information on the map.

Example:

Question: What is the distance between Vancouver and Calgary?

Answer: 1057 kilometres.

62

Map B

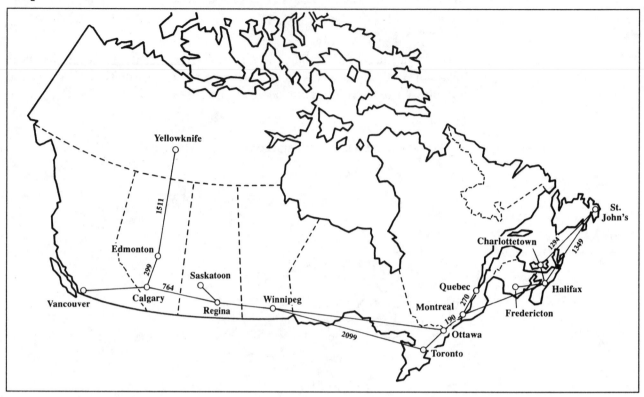

How Do I Get There?

> **Listening Activity 7**

Exercise 1: Get Ready to Listen

☐ ☐ Read these questions aloud with a partner. What do you think the story will be about?

1. The woman wants to go:

   a) from Edmonton to Vancouver

   b) from Vancouver to Edmonton

   c) from Winnipeg to Vancouver

2. To go by plane costs:

   a) $350

   b) $250

   c) $150

3. The flight takes:

a) an hour and 40 minutes

b) an hour and 20 minutes

c) an hour

4. The train takes:

a) 3 hours

b) 13 hours

c) 31 hours

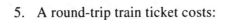

5. A round-trip train ticket costs:

a) $114

b) $134

c) $144

6. By car, the trip takes:

a) 9 hours

b) 11 hours

c) 21 hours

7. When you travel by car you:

a) go more quickly

b) see the countryside

c) pay more money

Exercise 2: Listen for Meaning

Listen to the conversation on the tape. What is the conversation about?

Exercise 3: Listen for Details

Go back to the questions. While you listen, choose the correct answers.

Exercise 4: Listen for Details Again

Make a chart similar to the one on page 64. While you listen, fill in the chart. If you have no information, put an ✗.

	Time	Cost
Plane		
Train		
Car		

What do you think is the best way for this woman to travel?

_____

◯ ◯   **Exercise 5: Listen for Sounds**

While you listen, write the missing words.

How Do I Get There?

Travel agent: Good morning. What can I do for you?

Woman: Well, I want to take a trip. I'm going to Vancouver. What'_____ the best way to get there?

Travel agent: Hmmm, let_____ see. From Edmonton to Vancouver is 1244 kilometres. You can go by car, by train or by plane. The fastest way is by plane.

Woman: By plane? How much does it cost?

Travel agent: It's $250 round trip. The flight _____ an hour and 20 minutes.

Woman: Wow, that'_____ expensive. How about by train? How long does it take by train?

Travel agent: The train takes about 13 hours. It costs $72 one way. That's $144 round trip.

Woman: Well, at least it's not as expensive.

Travel agent: Yes, and if you travel during the week, it's 40 percent off.

Woman: That sounds good. Are there any other ways _____ go?

Travel agent: You _____ drive. It takes about 11 hours. The gas won't be too expensive. That way you can see the countryside. It's very beautiful driving through the Rockies.

Woman: It would be nice to see the Rockies, but I might be tired from all that driving. I'll think about it _____ call you tomorrow.

Travel agent: That's fine. Be sure to book early if you take the train. It fills up quickly.

Exercise 6: Review Expressions

Match the expressions:

round trip	the price is 40 percent lower
40 percent off	buy your ticket soon
book early	the tickets sell quickly
fills up quickly	a two-way ticket

Exercise 7: Practise Speaking

Practise reading the dialogue with a partner. Then change roles and read it again.

Buying a Ticket

Role Play

Partner A

You are a traveller. You want to visit another city in Canada. Tell the travel agent where you are, and where you want to go.

Partner B

You are a travel agent. Tell the traveller some ways he or she can travel. Talk about distance, time and cost.

Both Partners

Decide on the travel plan. Write out the dialogue together. Act out your dialogue for the class.

Unit 9

Trees in Canada

Maple Trees
Reading

Maple Syrup
Listening Activity 8

Scrambled Colours
Spelling

Pine Trees
Reading

How a Pine Tree Grows
Interaction
Writing

Pines and Maples
Crossword Puzzle

Maple Trees

Exercise 1: Get Ready to Read

Work with a partner. Look at the picture.

1. What is the name of this leaf?
2. Where do we see it?
3. What kind of tree does it grow on?
4. Where do we see this kind of tree?
5. What products do we get from this tree?
6. What happens to this leaf in the autumn?

Exercise 2: Read Quickly for General Ideas

Maple Trees

Canada has many kinds of trees. One tree that is famous is the maple tree. Its leaf is Canada's national symbol. There is a picture of the maple leaf on the Canadian penny and on the Canadian flag.

The maple tree is very useful. We can use the wood from the maple tree to make many different things, such as household items and musical instruments. The colour of the wood is reddish-brown. The wood is very hard, so it is good for making furniture such as chairs, tables and dressers. It is especially good for making floors.

We get maple syrup from the maple tree. Maple syrup is a golden brown syrup that tastes delicious. It is made from sap, a liquid in the tree. We also get maple sugar from the sap. When the sap is dried, it can be made into candy.

The maple tree is also useful for small animals. It has seeds that fall to the ground and provide food for squirrels, birds and other small animals.

The maple tree is very tall. It grows to about 45 metres. The trunk is about a metre across. The most special thing about the maple tree is the way it changes. In the winter, the maple tree has no leaves. In spring, new leaves start to grow. In summer, the leaves are green. In the autumn, the leaves change colours before they fall off the trees. The leaves turn red, orange and yellow. The colours are very beautiful.

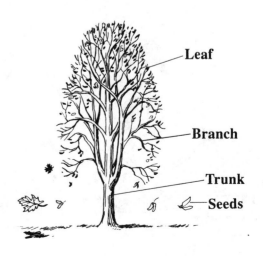

Exercise 3: Read Carefully for Details

Work with a partner. Look for the answers in the text.

1. Why is the maple tree famous in Canada?

2. Where can we see pictures of the maple leaf?

3. Name three things we can make from the wood of the maple tree.

4. Why is the wood good for making furniture?

5. Name two things we get from the sap of the maple tree.

6. How is the maple tree useful for birds and animals?

7. How high can a maple tree grow? How wide?

8. What happens to the maple leaves in each season?

   a) winter   c) summer

   b) spring   d) autumn

Maple Syrup

> **Listening Activity 8**

Exercise 1: Get Ready to Listen

☐☐ **A.** Work with a partner. Look at the pictures.

1. How do you eat maple syrup?

2. Which province is famous for maple syrup?

3. How do farmers get maple syrup from the trees?

B. Read these questions aloud with a partner. Then say what you think the story will be about.

1. Maple syrup is:

   a) a fruit

   b) a liquid

   c) a tree

2. Maple syrup tastes:

   a) sweet

   b) sour

   c) salty

3. People like to eat maple syrup:

   a) on pancakes

   b) as a drink

   c) on holidays

4. Which province produces the most maple syrup in the world?

   a) Manitoba

   b) Nova Scotia

   c) Quebec

5. Put these steps in order. The farmer:

   a) puts a spout in the hole

   b) puts a bucket under the spout

   c) cooks the sap to make syrup

   d) cuts a hole in the tree

6. The best time for maple syrup is:

   a) spring

   b) fall

   c) summer

7. Which foods can you eat at the farm?

   a) eggs

   b) bacon

   c) hamburgers

   d) cheese

   e) pancakes

   f) apples

8. Maple candy is made by putting the syrup:

   a) in a pot

   b) on a stove

   c) on the snow

Exercise 2: Listen for Meaning

Listen to the story on the tape. What is the story about?

 ## Exercise 3: Listen for Details

Go back to the questions. While you listen, choose the correct answers.

Exercise 4: Practise Writing

Write out the steps the farmer follows to make maple syrup.

Scrambled Colours

Write the letters your teacher dictates. Then work with a partner to unscramble the letters and find the names of the colours.

Pine Trees

Exercise 1: Get Ready to Read

☐ ☐ Work with a partner. Look at the picture of the tree.

1. What is special about this tree?

2. Why is it called evergreen?

3. What kind of leaves does it have?

4. What is a special time of the year when many people in Canada use this tree?

Exercise 2: Read Quickly for General Ideas

Pine Trees

The pine tree is a special kind of tree that grows in Canada. Some people call the pine tree a Christmas tree. This is because many people put pine trees in their homes at Christmas time. They decorate the tree with coloured lights, and put Christmas presents under the tree.

Pine trees are different from other trees because most other trees lose their leaves in the winter. Pine trees stay green all year long, even in the winter. Pine trees are also called evergreens because they are always green.

Pine trees do not have soft leaves like the maple tree. They have hard, thin leaves called needles. Pine trees also have pine cones. Pine cones look like hard berries. If you walk in a forest, you will see many pine cones on the ground. Inside the pine cones are seeds. When the seeds fall to the ground, a new tree starts to grow.

Pine trees grow everywhere in Canada. They are valuable trees for many reasons. The wood is used to make furniture and boats. Many kinds of birds build their nests in pine trees. The seeds of pine trees are food for small animals such as squirrels, chipmunks and mice and for bigger animals such as rabbits and black bears. The needles are good food for large animals such as deer and moose when they cannot find anything to eat in the winter.

If you walk in a forest of pine trees, the air has a wonderful pine scent. In winter, the white snow on the dark green trees looks very beautiful.

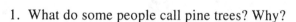

 ## Exercise 3: Read Carefully for Details

Work with a partner. Look in the text for the answers.

1. What do some people call pine trees? Why?

2. How are pine trees different from other trees?

3. Why are pine trees called evergreens?

4. What are the leaves of evergreens called?

5. What is inside pine cones?

6. What is the wood from pine trees used for?

7. Name some animals that eat the seeds of pine trees.

8. When do deer and moose eat the needles of pine trees?

9. What can you smell when you walk in a forest of pine trees?

10. Why does the pine tree look beautiful in winter?

How a Pine Tree Grows

☐☐   Work with a partner. Look at the pictures.

A. Match the sentences to the pictures. Start with 1 = C.

B. Write the sentences in the correct order.

Young trees are small and thin.

Pine trees often grow side by side.

1. Inside the pinecones are seeds.

The seeds fall to the ground. Some seeds grow into new trees.

Older trees have big trunks.

People cut some trees to use as Christmas trees.

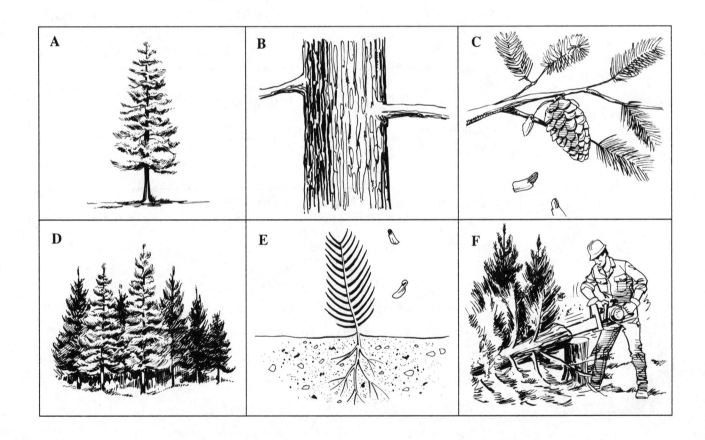

Pines and Maples

Crossword Puzzle

Across

3. Pine trees don't have leaves. They have ____.

5. The ____ leaf is the symbol of Canada.

7. We put maple ____ on our pancakes.

8. We make ____ from the wood of maple trees.

10. In the autumn, leaves change colours. They turn red, orange and ____.

12. One kind of evergreen tree is a ____ tree.

13. In summer, the colour of maple leaves is ____.

Down

1. Many people bring pine trees into their homes at ____ time.

2. Children like to eat ____ made from maple syrup.

4. The best season for maple syrup is ____.

6. The maple ____ changes colour in the autumn.

7. Birds and small animals eat the ____ from trees.

9. Pine trees and maple trees can grow very ____.

11. In ____, there are no leaves on the maple tree.

Unit 10

Pets

Why We Have Pets

Exercise 1: Get Ready to Read

Work in a group. Look at the picture of people with their pets.

1. Name some pets that people have.

2. Which animals make good pets? Why?

3. What pets do you think are popular in Canada?

Exercise 2: Read Quickly for General Ideas

Why We Have Pets

A pet is an animal that lives in your house. Over half the families in North America own pets. The most popular pets are dogs, cats, fish and birds. Rabbits, hamsters and turtles are also popular. Even some unpopular animals such as frogs, mice and snakes are pets.

People first started to keep pets about 12 000 years ago. The first pet was a dog. The dog did not become a pet because people thought it was cute. It became a pet because it was useful. People used the dog for many things. The dog warned people of danger. It also ate leftover food so wild animals didn't attack people. Later, dogs helped people take care of cows and sheep on farms.

Cats did not become pets for a long time. When the Egyptians first started to grow grain, mice ate it. The cats protected the grain. The Egyptians were the first to tame cats.

Today, people keep many kinds of pets. Animals such as canaries, parrots, mice and hamsters live in cages. They need people to bring them food and water and to keep their cages clean. Other animals, such as dogs and cats, need food and water but they can take care of themselves in many ways. They are good pets for people because they don't need much care.

Many people choose pets that are useful. For example, people use dogs to protect their homes. Dogs also help people who are blind or deaf or who can't use their arms or legs. Dogs are used in hunting, and they protect farm animals.

People have pets for different reasons, but most people have pets for pleasure. Pets are good friends for people, especially for children and older people.

Exercise 3: Read Carefully for Details

Work with a partner. Look for the answers in the text.

1. What is a pet?

2. Name three popular pets.

3. Name some other animals that people keep as pets.

4. When did people start to keep pets?

5. Which animal was the first pet?

6. Name three ways that dogs were useful to people.

7. Why did people keep cats as pets?

8. Name some animals that live in cages.

9. How do people take care of animals in cages?

10. Why are dogs and cats good pets?

11. Name four ways that people use dogs to help them.

12. Why do most people have pets?

Exercise 4: Review Vocabulary

☐☐ Work with a partner. Look at the list of pets. Write the name of the pet for each question. You can write some animals more than once.

cat   frog   turtle   bird   rabbit   dog

Example: Which pet can bring your newspaper into your house?   **dog**

Which pet can:

1. sing a song for you?

2. catch a mouse in your house?

3. hide in its shell?

4. guard your house when you go out?

5. catch flies in your house?

6. eat your leftover food?

Canaries

Choose the correct word for each space.

pets   home   name   birds   songs   sailors

Canaries are pretty yellow _____. They sing beautiful _____, and they are
           1   2

very popular as _____. Canaries get their _____ from the Canary Islands, near
                 3   4

Africa. They first became pets in the 1400s. Spanish _____ heard the canaries
                                                             5

sing, and liked their songs. They liked the songs so much that they took the

birds _____ to Spain.
    6

Buying a Pet

Listening Activity 9

Exercise 1: Get Ready to Listen

☐☐ **A.** Work with a partner. Look at the picture of the pet shop.

1. Name some animals you can buy in a pet shop.

2. Name some other products you can buy in a pet shop.

☐☐ **B.** Read these questions aloud with a partner. What do you think this conversation will be about?

1. Andrea wants to buy:

   a) a pet

   b) pet food

   c) a plant

2. Andrea already has:
   a) a dog
   b) a frog
   c) a turtle

3. Andrea says goldfish:
   a) are fun to play with
   b) aren't fun to play with
   c) are free

4. Andrea doesn't want a kitten because:
   a) her father doesn't like them
   b) her brother hates them
   c) her mother doesn't like them

5. Andrea doesn't want a bird because:
   a) they are pretty
   b) they are expensive
   c) they are noisy

6. Andrea wants another turtle because:
   a) they are not expensive
   b) her turtle is lonely
   c) she is lonely

⊙⊙ Exercise 2: Listen for Meaning

Listen to the conversation. What is the conversation about?

⊙⊙ Exercise 3: Listen for Details

Go back to the questions. While you listen, choose the correct answers.

⊙⊙ Exercise 4: Listen for Sounds

While you listen, write the missing words.

Buying a Pet

Sales clerk: Hello, can I help you?

Andrea: Yes, I want _____ buy a pet.

Sales clerk: OK. What kind _____ pet would you like?

Andrea: Oh boy, oh boy, oh boy. Well, I already have a turtle. So I guess I would like something bigger.

Sales clerk: Something bigger, eh? How about _____ dog? Would you like a dog?

Andrea: No. A dog is too big. And you have _____ take a dog for a walk every day. A dog is too much work.

Sales clerk: How about a goldfish? Goldfish _____ small. And you don't have to take them for a walk.

Andrea: That's true. But goldfish _____ no fun to play with. They just swim around all day.

Sales clerk: Well, what about _____ cat? Or a kitten? Our mother cat just had babies. We have some cute kittens.

Andrea: Well, I guess kittens _____ cute. But I don't really like kittens that much. And my mother doesn't like them.

Sales clerk: How about a bird then? Birds _____ sing for you. And they are pretty to look at.

Andrea: Yes, they are pretty. But I hate to clean the bird's cage. And they make _____ lot of noise.

Sales clerk: How about a rabbit?

Andrea: No.

Sales clerk: A hamster?

Andrea: Uh uh.

Sales clerk: A mouse?

Andrea: Yuch.

Sales clerk: A snake?

Andrea: Never!

Sales clerk: Well, what do you want?

Andrea: A turtle.

Sales clerk: A turtle? But you already have _____ turtle.

Andrea: I know. But my turtle'_____ lonely. She needs a friend. And I really like turtles best.

Exercise 5: Practise Speaking

Practise reading the dialogue with a partner. Then change roles and read it again.

What About You?

Discuss these questions in a group.

1. Do you have a pet? What kind?
2. Did you have a pet when you were young? What kind?
3. What kinds of pets are popular in other countries?
4. Which animals do you think make the best pets? Why?
5. Do dogs and cats live in the house in other countries?

Taking a Walk

Choose the correct word for each space.

poet   owners   lobster   dog   pets

Most pet owners love their _____ very much. Some pet _____ like to show off
                            1   2
their pets. The French _____ Baudelaire liked to show off his pet. He used to
                        3
take it for a walk. But Baudelaire's pet was not a _____. It was a _____!
                                                   4   5

A Perfect Pet

Role Play

Partner A

You want to buy a pet. You go to the pet store to choose a pet. You ask about different pets. Ask questions about how to take care of the animals, what to feed them, etc.

Partner B

You work in a pet shop. The customer asks you questions about different animals. Help the customer decide what to buy.

Both Partners

Discuss different pets, and decide on the best one for the customer. Write your dialogue. Be prepared to act it out for the class.

Popular Pets

Crossword Puzzle

Across

5. A _____ is a pet that swims in a bowl.

7. A canary is a pretty bird. Its colour is _____.

8. A pet is an animal that lives in your _____.

9. A _____ is a small animal that has a shell.

10. _____ are popular pets. They have four legs, and a long tail.

11. A bird is a nice pet. It can _____ a song for you.

12. Dogs can be useful pets. Some dogs help _____ people.

Down

1. A baby cat is called a _____.

2. Cats catch _____.

3. When a turtle is afraid, it can hide in its _____.

4. Some people keep dogs for _____. The dogs keep them safe.

6. Dogs, cats and birds are the most _____ pets.

13. If you leave your pet alone for a long time, it will feel _____.

14. A _____ is a very popular pet.

Sports

Hockey

Exercise 1: Get Ready to Read

Look at the picture. Work in a group to answer the questions.

1. In which countries do people play hockey?
2. Where do people go to play hockey?
3. How do you play?
4. What equipment do you need?

Exercise 2: Read Quickly for General Ideas

Hockey

Hockey is one of Canada's favourite sports. Every year thousands of Canadians play hockey or watch hockey on television. Hockey is also popular in other places, such as the United States, Japan, Russia and western Europe. Hockey became an Olympic sport in 1920.

Hockey is a fast, rough game. Professional teams play in large arenas. The players skate very fast on the ice. They try to score goals. They use a hockey stick to hit a puck. A puck is like a ball, but it is flat. To score a goal, the hockey players hit the puck into a net.

Sometimes the players hit each other. Then, sometimes, they fall down and slide on the ice. Hockey players wear special equipment for protection. They wear heavy sweaters, pants and gloves. They wear helmets to protect their heads.

Many children play hockey in the winter. Children often play outside. Many cities build skating rinks in the park. In the country, children can play hockey on frozen ponds, lakes or rivers. Children who play on teams usually wear the same equipment as professional players. Hockey is rough and they need protection.

Long ago, all hockey games were played outside. Everyone played on frozen rivers and lakes. In the spring there were sometimes accidents when players fell through the ice. Today, people often play in indoor arenas. They don't have to stop playing when the weather gets warm.

Exercise 3: Review Vocabulary

Work with a partner. Find the words in the text. Use the context to help you understand the meaning. Choose the best answer.

1. A **professional** player means:

    a) good

    b) paid

    c) adult

2. They try to **score goals** means:

    a) make points

    b) skate faster

    c) win the game

3. They **slide** on the ice means:

    a) skate very quickly

    b) sit down hard

    c) move without trying

4. They wear hockey **equipment** means:

    a) clothes

    b) uniforms

    c) special things they need for protection

5. The city builds **rinks** in the park means:

    a) snow castles

    b) outside arenas

    c) special games

6. It's a **rough** game means:
   a) fast
   b) fun
   c) hard

7. On the **frozen** rivers means:
   a) cold
   b) icy
   c) small

Exercise 4: Read Carefully for Details

Work with a partner. Look in the text for the answers.

1. Canadians like hockey.   **T** (true) or **F** (false)?

2. Name some other places where hockey is popular.

3. Where do people play hockey?

4. Where do they hit the puck to score a goal?

5. What happens when players hit each other?

6. Why do hockey players need to wear special equipment?

7. Name some clothing and equipment that hockey players wear.

8. When do children play hockey?

9. Where do children play hockey:
   a) in the city?
   b) in the country?

10. What do children wear to play hockey?

11. Where was hockey played in the past?

12. What kind of accident happened in the spring?

13. Why do people like to play hockey in indoor arenas?

Is It "z" or "s"?

Practise Pronunciation

With a long vowel sound use **z**
   Example: eyes

With a short vowel sound use **s**
   Example: ice

Write the word the teacher says:

1. pays   pace
2. place   plays
3. rice   rise
4. price   prize
5. desert   dessert
6. lose   loose
7. bus   buzz

Kinds of Sport

Exercise 1: Get Ready

Work in a group. Look at the sports equipment in the pictures. Choose the name of the sport for each piece of equipment.

badminton
baseball
basketball
boxing
football
fishing
golf
hiking
hockey
jogging
judo
skating
skiing
soccer
weight lifting

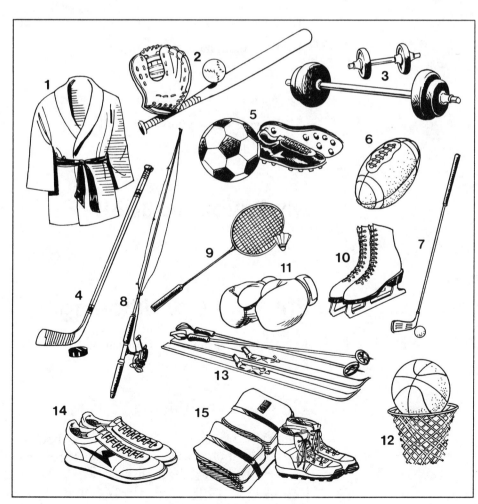

Exercise 2: Review Vocabulary

☐☐ Make a chart similar to the one below. Write the name of each sport in one or more categories.

Team Sport	Individual Sport	Physical Conditioning

What About You?

☐☐ Choose your favourite sport from the list on page 87. Describe the sport to your partner. Here is some information to give:

1. What do you wear?

2. What equipment do you use?

3. Where do you play?

4. What is the best season for your sport?

5. Do you play it yourself?

6. Why do you like it?

My Favourite Sport

Write about your favourite sport.

Physical Conditioning

Read this paragraph for information. Then list five reasons that sports are good for us.

Physical Conditioning

One reason we do sports is to make our bodies strong and healthy. Exercise helps build strong muscles. It is also good for our hearts and for our lungs. Another good thing about physical activity is that it helps us to relax. Finally, taking part in sports is a good way to meet other people.

Where Do We Get in Shape?

Exercise 1: Get Ready

Work with a partner. Look at the pictures of some places we do sports. Name each place.

at the park   **in the mountains**

on the water   **in the pool**

in the gym   **on a playing field**

Exercise 2: Use the Information

Write the names of the sports we do in each place. We can do some sports in more than one place.

badminton	football	sailing
baseball	gymnastics	skiing
basketball	soccer	swimming
diving	hiking	tai chi
fishing	jogging	water skiing

Exercise 3: Practise Spelling

Spell these words. Fill in the missing letters.

h_ckey	hi_ing	pl_yer	swi_ming	ski_ng
eq_i_ment	ph_si_al	jo_ _ing	s_ating	te_m

Sports Talk

Crossword Puzzle

Across

2. Hockey players don't play hockey in summer. They play in ____.
5. Canada's national sport is ____.
6. Hockey players use a ____ to hit a puck.
9. Many Canadians like to go ice ____ in winter.
11. You can swim in a lake or in a ____.
12. People lift weights to build bigger ____.
13. What sports do you like to ____?

Down

1. Some people like to catch ____ as a sport.
3. Hockey players play hockey in a ____.
4. A popular American sport is ____.
7. People skate on frozen rivers and ____.
8. To play ____, players hit a ball with a bat.
10. You can do gymnastics and other sports in a ____.
11. You can run or play ball outside in a ____.

Department Stores

The Department Store
Interaction

Department Stores in Canada
Reading
Cultural Information

Pay at the Cash
Listening Activity 10

The West Edmonton Mall
Vocabulary

Buying on Sale
Reading
Interaction
Cultural Information

What About You?
Discussion

The Department Store

Work in a group. Look at the picture of the department store. Write the name of the department where you can find each item. You can find some things in more than one place. Write all the places.

1. a winter jacket
2. a refrigerator
3. a man's jacket
4. a radio
5. a gift for a new baby
6. a lamp for your living room
7. a tennis racket
8. a dress for your sister
9. towels
10. a record for your friend's birthday
11. a hammer and nails
12. an umbrella
13. a tie for your uncle
14. a gift for your father on Father's Day
15. a sweater for a child
16. a gift for your mother on Mother's Day
17. a washing machine
18. a bed
19. winter boots
20. a tent to go camping

Department Stores in Canada

Exercise 1: Read Quickly for General Ideas

Department Stores in Canada

When you go shopping for furniture or clothes in Canada, where do you go? One place you can go is a department store. A department store is like many small stores under one roof. Department stores such as Eaton's, the Bay and Sears have been in Canada for a long time.

Long ago people traded with each other to get the clothes and food they needed. In Canada, special places were set up for trading. These places were called trading posts. Later, when people began using money to buy things, people shopped in general stores. These stores had food, clothing, fabric to make clothes, tools and even furniture.

When cities got bigger, the stores became bigger too. They had separate places, or departments, for different things. The customers were happy, because they didn't have to walk to many different stores to buy the things they needed.

When department stores started in Canada, people's way of shopping changed. In the past, at a trading post or general store, there was no set price for goods. When people wanted to buy something, they bargained with the owner, and tried to pay the lowest price. In department stores, this changed. There were fixed prices for everything in the store. Everyone paid the same price.

The next thing that changed was that people paid right away. In general stores, people knew the owners. If they did not have enough money to buy something, they could pay a little at a time. Department stores were much bigger than general stores. The owner did not know all the customers, so everyone had to pay when they bought something.

The department store was different in another way. If you were not happy with something you bought in the department store, you could return it and get your money back. This was the first time people had this guarantee.

Exercise 2: Read Carefully for Details

Work with a partner. Look in the text for the answers.

1. Name some department stores in Canada.

2. In the past, how did people get things they needed?

3. What is a trading post?

4. When people began to use money, where did they shop?

5. Name some things you could buy in a general store.

6. When did stores become bigger?

7. What are departments?

8. Why do customers like to shop in department stores?

9. How did people decide on a price in the past?

10. What was different about prices in a department store?

11. What happened if people did not have enough money in a general store?

12. How did people have to pay for things in department stores?

13. What guarantee did the department store give?

Pay at the Cash

Listening Activity 10

Exercise 1: Get Ready to Listen

Read these questions aloud with a partner. What do you think the information will be about?

1. In a department store, where do you pay?
    a) on the sidewalk
    b) at the nearest cash
    c) in the aisle

2. People think you want to steal things if:
    a) you pay for them
    b) you walk around with them
    c) you ask for help with them

3. What does the cashier do when you pay for something?
    a) gives you your money back
    b) lines up at the cash
    c) gives you a receipt

4. You can pay for something in a department store with:
    a) a credit card
    b) a sales slip
    c) a receipt

5. If you have a problem with something that you buy, you can:
    a) line up at the cash
    b) use a credit card
    c) get your money back

6. "Final sale" means:

    a) you are too early

    b) you cannot get your money back

    c) there is nothing left to buy

○○ Exercise 2: Listen for Meaning

Listen to the information. What is the information about?

○○ Exercise 3: Listen for Details

Go back to the questions. While you listen, choose the correct answers.

The West Edmonton Mall

Choose the correct word for each space.

world   people   week   stores   centre

The West Edmonton Mall in Alberta is the largest shopping _____ in the
1

_____. It has over 800 _____. It also has many services, such as amusement
2 3

parks, aquariums, movie theatres, a hotel, a skating rink, a water park and

more. Sixteen thousand _____ work at the West Edmonton Mall. Every _____,
4 5

half a million people shop there.

Buying on Sale

Exercise 1: Get Ready to Read

□□ Work with a partner. Look at the picture. What do you think the people are doing? Why?

Exercise 2: Read Quickly for General Ideas

Buying on Sale

When you buy things in other countries, do you bargain for the best price? In Canada, you generally can't bargain for a better price, especially in a department store. Instead, Canadians "look for bargains." This means they try to find the best price for something they want to buy. For example, if they need a new coat, they go to a few stores and look at the prices before they decide what to buy.

Stores in Canada have sales a few times a year. When they have sales, the prices are lower. You can find out about sales in the newspaper or from advertising flyers.

Stores usually have sales at the end of the season. They reduce the prices near the end of the season to make room for new merchandise. For example, in January, all the winter clothes go on sale. You can buy a winter coat for much less money than it would cost in September or October. This is the same for summer clothes. Bathing suits usually go on sale in July.

Stores have sales at other times as well. Stores sometimes have sales after holidays or on special occasions, such as the store's anniversary. Sometimes they have clearance sales. This means that a store buys a big stock of certain items, such as raincoats in the spring or sheets and towels in January. Then the store puts the items on sale so that they will sell quickly.

When you buy on sale, you have to be careful. Just because something is on sale does not mean it is a bargain. Be sure it is something that you really need, and be sure to check the item carefully. Perhaps it is damaged or out of style. Usually you cannot return something that you buy on sale.

Before you buy something, ask yourself why the item is on sale. By watching the ads and checking items carefully, a smart shopper can save a lot of money by buying things on sale.

Exercise 3: Read Carefully for Details

Work with a partner. Look in the text for the answers.

1. In Canada, can you ask for a lower price in a department store?
2. What does it mean to "look for a bargain"? Give an example.
3. What happens to prices when stores have sales?
4. Name two places you can find out about sales.
5. When do most stores have sales?
6. Why do stores reduce prices at the end of the season?
7. When can you buy a winter coat on sale?
8. When can you buy a bathing suit on sale?
9. Name two other times stores have sales.
10. What is a clearance sale?
11. What should you check before you buy something on sale?
12. How can a smart shopper save money?

Exercise 4: Transfer Information

Work with a partner. Make a chart similar to the one below. Look at the information on page 99. Find the best time to buy clothes and other items you need on sale. Write the months in the chart.

School supplies			
A second-hand car			
New winter boots			
Sheets and towels			
A bracelet			
A couch			
A man's shirt			
Shorts for the summer			
A gift for a young child			
A suitcase			
A camera			
A tie			

Sales

January:

dresses

toys

white sales

cards

wrapping paper

Christmas decorations

winter clothes

winter boots

February:

winter clothes

winter boots

bedding

furniture

March:

dishes

luggage

tires

April:

children's clothes

men's suits

spring coats

women's stockings

May:

television sets

towels

June:

men's and boys' clothes

dresses

July:

men's shirts

summer clothes

summer shoes

bathing suits

August:

back-to-school clothes

notebooks

writing paper

pens and pencils

September:

new cars

furniture

rugs

October:

handicrafts

dishes

lamps

November:

used cars

blankets

December:

men's clothes

cameras

jewellery

books

What About You?

Discuss these questions in a group.

1. Are there large department stores in most countries? Name some department stores in Canada or other countries.

2. Do you line up at the cash to pay in all countries?

3. How do you usually pay for things in a department store: cash, cheque or credit card?

4. Can you bargain for a better price in department stores outside Canada?

5. Do stores in other countries have sales? When are the sales?

6. Do you prefer to shop in a department store or in smaller stores? Why?

7. Are things more expensive in department stores or in small stores in other countries? Where is clothing more expensive: in other countries or in Canada?

Going Out

Tipping
Interaction
Reading
Cultural Information

Reservations at the Restaurant
Listening Activity 11

Going Out to Eat
Role Play

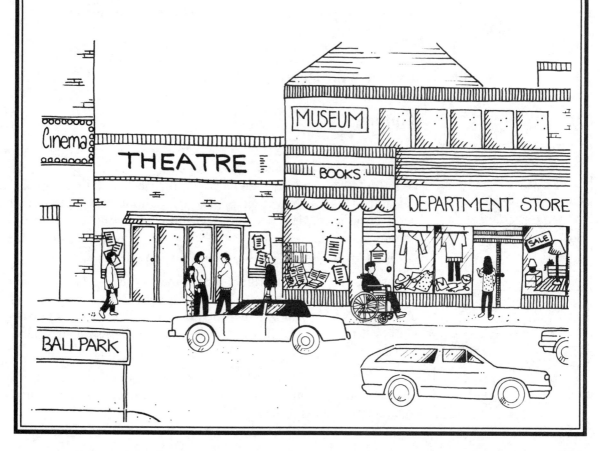

Tipping

Exercise 1: Get Ready to Read

Discuss these questions in a group.

1. Which people do you tip in different countries?

2. How much tip do you leave?

3. In Canada, who do you tip? Choose the people you think you should tip.

    a) hairdresser

    b) delivery person

    c) teacher

    d) office worker

    e) taxi driver

    f) bus driver

    g) police officer

    h) bank teller

    i) dentist

    j) waiter

4. What do you think happens if you tip the wrong person?

Exercise 2: Read Quickly for General Information

Tipping

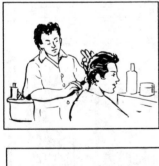

A tip is a service charge that you leave for good service. Usually a tip is 10 to 15 percent of the bill. In some places you don't leave a tip. For example, you don't tip teachers. It can even be an insult. They could think you are trying to get higher marks. Never tip a professional, such as your doctor or your dentist, and never tip a police officer. In other places you do leave a tip. It's an error not to tip in a restaurant where you sit at the table to be served. Here are some rules about where and how to tip in Canada.

Generally, you tip the hairdresser or barber when you have a haircut. It is a good idea to leave the money quietly near the hairdresser's work station. You also tip in a taxi. You pay the taxi fare. The driver gives you change. Then you hand the driver a tip. As you put the tip in the driver's hand, you say "Thank you."

Other people you tip are ushers in nightclubs and porters at airports and railway stations. You can also tip the person who cleans your room in a hotel. You do this when you check out.

Restaurants are places where you often tip, but you don't tip in all restaurants. The rule is that when you serve yourself and carry food to your table, you don't tip. When you sit and someone comes to the table and serves you, you tip. In the restaurant you leave the money on the table. It isn't polite to hand the money to waiters or waitresses. Also, they need to pay attention to serving other customers.

 Exercise 3: Read Carefully for Details

Work with a partner. Look in the text for the answers.

1. Look at these bills. How much do you leave as a tip?

   a) restaurant bill: $16.85

   b) taxi: $5.40

   c) restaurant bill: $43.28

   d) haircut: $32.00

   e) taxi: $9.60

2. What can happen if you tip the wrong person?

3. You hand money to the hairdresser as a tip.   **T** (true) or **F** (false)?

4. You are getting out of a taxi. Put the steps in the right order.

   a) You say thank you.

   b) The driver gives you change.

   c) You tip the driver.

   d) You pay the taxi fare.

   e) The driver tells you the price.

5. When do you tip the person who cleans your room in a hotel?

6. When do you not tip in a restaurant?

7. When do you tip in a restaurant?

8. Where do you leave the tip in a restaurant?

9. Give two reasons why you don't hand money to the waiter or waitress.

Reservations at the Restaurant

Exercise 1: Get Ready to Listen

Before you begin, cover Exercise 4 on page 105.

Read these questions aloud with a partner. What do you think the conversation will be about?

1. What time of day does this conversation take place?

    a) morning

    b) afternoon

    c) evening

2. What does the man want to reserve?

    a) a table for six

    b) six tables

    c) dinner at six

3. What time is the reservation for?

    a) 6 o'clock

    b) 8 o'clock

    c) 10 o'clock

4. Where does the man want to sit?

    a) at the counter

    b) near the window

    c) beside the door

5. What day of the week is the reservation for?

    a) Thursday

    b) Tuesday

    c) Friday

6. Who is having a birthday?

    a) the man

    b) his sister

    c) his brother

7. What does the man order?

    a) a box of chocolates

    b) some mocha coffee

    c) a chocolate cake

8. What is the man's name?

   a) Mr. Ray

   b) Mr. Grey

   c) Mr. Gray

9. Where will the man park his car?

   a) behind the restaurant

   b) in a parking lot

   c) on the street

⊙⊙ Exercise 2: Listen for Meaning

Listen to the conversation. What is the conversation about?

⊙⊙ Exercise 3: Listen for Details

Go back to the questions. While you listen, choose the correct answers.

⊙⊙ Exercise 4: Listen for Sounds

While you listen, write the missing words.

Reservations at the Restaurant

Restaurant owner:	Good afternoon. Giovanni's Restaurant. Can I help you?
Customer:	Yes. ____ like to make reservations for six people for Thursday evening.
Restaurant owner:	Certainly sir. We ____ reserve a table for six people. What time do you to want ____ dine?
Customer:	Oh, I guess around 8 o'clock. Can you reserve the table near the window?
Restaurant owner:	Yes sir. Let me check. You want to reserve a table for six near the window. ____ 8 o'clock. What day do you want?
Customer:	Next Thursday. It's my sister's birthday.
Restaurant owner:	OK, no problem. Anything else sir?
Customer:	Yes. Can we have a birthday cake? Do ____ have birthday cakes?

Restaurant owner:	Yes, sir. We have excellent cakes. Our birthday cakes ____ chocolate or mocha.
Customer:	Chocolate would be fine.
Restaurant owner:	What ____ your name please?
Customer:	Michael Grey. That's G-R-E-Y.
Restaurant owner:	Certainly, Mr. Grey. Reservations for six, ____ 8 o'clock on Thursday, with a birthday cake.
Customer:	That's right. Thank you. Oh. ____ you have parking?
Restaurant owner:	No sir. But you can find ____ place to park on the street. It's not very busy on Thursday nights.
Customer:	Oh, good. Thank you. Goodbye.
Restaurant owner:	Goodbye.

Exercise 5: Practise Speaking

Practise reading the dialogue with a partner. Then change roles and read it again.

Going Out to Eat

Role Play

It is the last day of class. You are making plans to eat out in a restaurant.

Partner A

You want to make a reservation at a restaurant. Call the restaurant to make a reservation. Be ready to say the day, the time and the number of people in the group.

Partner B

You work at the restaurant. The customer calls to make a reservation. Ask about the day, the time and the number of people in the group.

Both Partners

Work together to write a dialogue. Be prepared to act it out for the class.

Unit 14

Do You Need a Doctor?

Getting Sick
Reading
Spelling

At the Doctor
Listening Activity 12

I Think I'm Catching a Cold
Vocabulary

Doctor, It Hurts
Role Play

Getting Sick

Exercise 1: Get Ready to Read

A. Work in a group. Look at the pictures. Match the problem to the picture.

headache	**sore knee**
backache	**stomachache**
sore throat	**toothache**
sore shoulder	**earache**

B. Read the questions aloud with a partner.

1. What happens when we aren't healthy?

2. What are two words that mean "hurt"?

3. What are aches?

4. Give some examples of aches.

5. What do we say to describe simple health problems that aren't called aches? Give examples.

6. When do we use the word "pain" to describe a problem?

7. What can we do for small aches?

8. When do we have to visit the doctor?

9. What are three things the doctor can do in order to know what is wrong?

Exercise 2: Read Carefully for Information

Read the text. **Then go back to the questions.** Work with a partner to find the answers.

Getting Sick

Nobody wants to be sick. Unfortunately our bodies can develop problems. When we aren't healthy, our bodies tell us. Sometimes a part of our body hurts. When a part of our body hurts, we say we have aches and pains. We can have aches and pains in different parts of the body.

We call some simple health problems "aches." For example, we can have a headache, a toothache, an earache, a backache or a stomachache. Other simple problems are not called aches, so we describe them in different ways. For example, we can have a sore throat, a sore leg, a sore toe.

"Pain" is another word that we use to describe a problem. We can have a pain in the chest, a pain in the shoulder or a pain in the back. A pain is strong. Also, a pain hurts in a specific place.

When aches and pains aren't too serious, we can buy medicine in the drugstore. Usually small aches go away quickly. When pain is more serious, we have to visit the doctor (or the dentist). The doctor asks us what our symptoms are. The doctor may have to do tests or take X-rays to know what is wrong. Then he or she will tell us what to do.

Exercise 3: Practise Spelling

Spell these words. Fill in the missing letters.

p_in   ac_e

he_lth   s_re

me_ic_ne   bod_es

doct_r   d_nt_st

s_mpt_ms   wr_ng

hu_t   to_th_che

mus_les   ser_ous

At the Doctor

> **Listening Activity 12**

Exercise 1: Get Ready to Listen

A. Work with a partner. Look at the pictures. Use the information below to help you name the parts inside the body.

The stomach digests the food.

The lungs are for breathing.

The throat is inside the neck.

The kidneys filter blood. They are in the back.

The liver breaks down food.

The appendix is a small organ below the stomach.

The heart pumps blood.

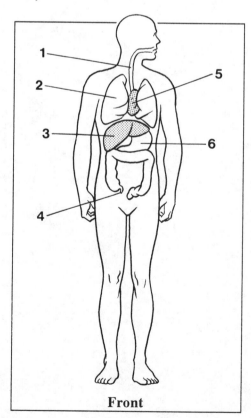

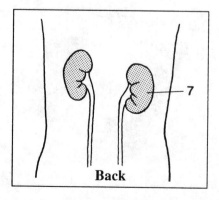

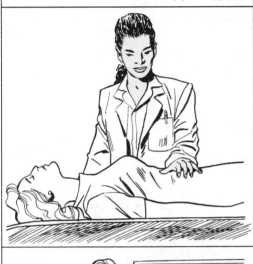

B. Read these questions aloud with a partner. Then say what you think the conversation will be about.

1. The patient is:
   a) feeling well
   b) in pain
   c) hungry

2. The patient thinks the problem is:
   a) her heart
   b) her lungs
   c) her liver

3. The doctor says the liver is:
   a) below the stomach
   b) near the stomach
   c) above the stomach

4. The patient feels pain:
   a) in the abdomen
   b) in the stomach
   c) on the left side

5. The kidneys are:
   a) in the back
   b) above the lungs
   c) on the right side

6. The doctor wants to:
   a) talk to the patient
   b) take an X-ray
   c) call the pharmacy

7. The doctor thinks that the problem may be:
   a) the kidneys
   b) the appendix
   c) the liver

Did You Know? In Canada, most people have a "family doctor." This doctor knows their medical history. When they have a medical problem, they call this doctor. Sometimes the family doctor will refer the patient to a specialist. The best way to choose a family doctor is to ask friends or neighbours for the name of a doctor they know.

⊡ Exercise 2: Listen for Meaning

Before you begin, cover Exercise 4.

Listen to the conversation. What is the conversation about?

⊡ Exercise 3: Listen for Details

Go back to the questions. While you listen, choose the correct answer.

⊡ Exercise 4: Listen for Sounds

While you listen, write the missing words.

At the Doctor

Doctor: What ____ I do for you? What's wrong?

Patient: I don't feel well, doctor. I'm ____ pain.

Doctor: What are your symptoms?

Patient: Pain. It hurts here. ____ either my stomach or my liver.

Doctor: Your liver? Show me where it hurts.

Patient: Here doctor. It hurts here.

Doctor: Hmmm. ____ not your liver. Your liver is above your stomach.

Patient: No, it's here doctor. ____ below my stomach.

Doctor: Your abdomen, you mean. That's not your stomach. That's your abdomen.

Patient: Yes, my abdomen. ____ the right. The pain is on the right side. Maybe it's my kidneys.

Doctor: Your kidneys are higher up. They are higher up and you have two. Your kidneys are in the back. It's not your kidneys.

Patient: What is it then Doctor? I have a lot of pain here.

Doctor: Well, I need ____ examine you. I need to do some tests too. Maybe I need to take an X-ray. Maybe ____ your appendix. You may need an operation.

Exercise 5: Practise Speaking

□ □ Practise reading the dialogue with a partner. Then change roles and read it again.

I Think I'm Catching a Cold

Choose the right word for each space.

cold   bed   weather   tired   throat   snow

It's winter in Canada. The ____ is cold and damp. There is ____ on the ground.
                    1   2

People in the bus sneeze and cough. I think I'm catching a ____. I have a sore
                                                3

____. I feel ____. My eyes are red. I think I'll go to ____.
4   5   6

Doctor, It Hurts

Role Play

Partner A

You are at the doctor's office. You are feeling sick. Describe how you feel. Tell the doctor what kind of ache or pain you have, and where it is.

Partner B

You are a doctor. A patient is in your office. The patient describes his or her aches and pains. Ask the patient questions about symptoms. Then suggest tests, X-rays, etc.

Both Partners

Together, write a dialogue. Be prepared to act it out for the class.

Animals

Animals in Different Countries
Interaction

Bears in North America
Reading

Polar Bears
Listening Activity 13

Pandas and Koalas
Reading

The Camel
Reading
Vocabulary
Spelling

How to Buy a Camel
Listening Activity 14

Animals in Different Countries

Work in a group. Look at the pictures of animals.

1. Name the animals.

2. Look at this list of animals. Can you name some countries where these animals live?

    squirrel beaver camel elephant mouse alligator parrot

    monkey moose eagle bear (what kind?) tiger gecko

    snake (what kind?) donkey goat cow chicken sheep ox

    shark octopus

3. Think of examples of the following:

    a) a bird

    b) a fish

    c) a farm animal

    d) a wild animal

    e) a pet

    f) a reptile

4. Draw pictures of the animals you used as examples.

Bears in North America

Exercise 1: Get Ready to Read

Work in a group. Read the questions and discuss them. Answer **T** (true) or **F** (false).

1. Bears live in Canada.

2. Bears can climb trees.

3. Bears eat plants.

4. Bears can weigh more than 700 kilograms.

5. Some bears hibernate (sleep) in the winter.

6. Bears can swim.

7. Bears can be dangerous to people.

Exercise 2: Read Quickly for General Ideas

Bears in North America

Bears live everywhere in North America. We see bears most often in zoos. People like them because they are playful and fun to watch.

Bears are large animals with heavy bodies and long shaggy fur. Bears can sometimes walk on their two back legs. Usually they walk on four legs. They can run very fast for short distances. Bears have sharp claws which they use to climb trees.

If you look at a bear you will see that it has small eyes. Bears don't see very well. They use their other senses more. They have a sharp sense of smell and good hearing.

The most common bears are brown or black. They weigh about 150 kilograms. These bears live in forests all over North America. They eat fruit, plants, fish and small animals. In winter they sleep in caves. They don't come outside before spring. Their cubs are born in the caves.

Polar bears live in the Arctic. They are white and they are very big. They aren't the biggest land animals. Elephants are, but polar bears are the biggest land animals that eat meat. Polar bears eat fish and seals that they catch in the ocean. They hunt for their food in the ocean and on the ice. They are very good swimmers.

Another big bear is the grizzly. This bear can weigh 500 kilograms. Grizzlies live in western North America. Grizzly bears live in the mountains and in the forests. They don't sleep in the winter. They hunt for food day and night, in all kinds of weather. They eat small animals, fish, plants and garbage. Grizzly bears are sometimes dangerous.

Exercise 3: Transfer Information

Make a chart similar to the one below. Work with a partner to complete the chart. If you have no information, put an ✗.

Bear	Brown or Black Bear	Polar Bear	Grizzly
Colour			
Weight			
Where it lives			
Food			
Sleep			
Special things it can do			

Exercise 4: Read Carefully for Details

A. Work with a partner. Look in the text for the answers.

1. Where do bears live?

2. Why do people like to watch bears?

3. Bears can walk on their back legs.   **T** (true) or **F** (false)?

4. Bears cannot move very fast.   **T F**

5. Bears can see and hear well.   **T F**

6. Name some foods that brown and black bears eat.

7. What do brown and black bears do in winter?

8. Polar bears are the biggest land animals.   **T F**

9. Polar bears are good swimmers.   **T F**

10. The grizzly bear is a big bear.   **T F**

11. Where do grizzlies live?

12. What do grizzlies eat?

13. Grizzly bears can be dangerous.   **T F**

B. Now go back to the prediction questions on page 116 and check the answers.

Exercise 5: Practise Grammar

List all the main verbs in the text. Don't list auxiliary verbs.

Polar Bears

(**Listening Activity 13**)

Exercise 1: Get Ready to Listen

Read these questions aloud with a partner.

1. What colour is a polar bear?

   a) brown

   b) white

   c) black

2. Polar bears live:

   a) in the North

   b) in the West

   c) in the South

3. The polar bear is hard to see because:

   a) it has white fur

   b) it is a small animal

   c) it swims in the ocean

4. The polar bear can stay under water:

   a) for three minutes

   b) for two minutes

   c) for five minutes

5. How far can polar bears swim?

   a) three kilometres

   b) hundreds of kilometres

   c) a few kilometres

6. The bear's paws help it to:

   a) walk on the snow

   b) hold its babies

   c) eat plants

7. Female polar bears sleep:

   a) in the spring

   b) in a cave

   c) in the ocean

8. Baby polar bears are born:

   a) in November

   b) in December

   c) in March

9. Who hunts for food?

   a) the father

   b) the mother

   c) the cubs

10. The cubs stay with their mother:

   a) for one year

   b) for two years

   c) for two and a half years

⊙⊙ Exercise 2: Listen for Meaning

Listen to the story. What is the story about?

⊙⊙ Exercise 3: Listen for Details

Go back to the questions. While you listen, choose the correct answer.

Exercise 4: Review Vocabulary

Match the opposites.

1. land   cold

2. black   summer

3. small   white

4. warm   easy

5. sleep   ocean

6. north   south

7. hard   wake up

8. winter   big

Pandas and Koalas

Exercise 1: Get Ready to Read

☐☐ Work with a partner. Look at the pictures of the panda and the koala.

1. Describe these animals.

2. Do you know where they live?

3. Do you know what they eat?

Exercise 2: Read Quickly for General Ideas

Pandas and Koalas

Pandas and koalas are two special animals. They are special because they look very beautiful, and people think they are cute and cuddly. There are many toys and stuffed animals that look like pandas and koalas. People sometimes call pandas and koalas bears, but they are not really bears.

The panda is a big animal with thick white fur on most of its body. It has black legs and ears. It has black on its shoulders and around its eyes. The panda lives in Tibet and south-west China. The panda eats plants, mostly bamboo shoots. It lives on the ground but it can climb trees.

The koala lives in Australia. It has a pouch like a kangaroo. The koala is a small animal with thick grey fur. It lives in trees. It sleeps all day and feeds at night. It has a strange smell, because it eats leaves from eucalyptus trees. These are the leaves we use to make cough medicine.

Sadly, both pandas and koalas are in danger. People have killed too many pandas and koalas. Soon there may be none left.

Exercise 3: Transfer Information

Make a chart similar to the one below. Compare the panda and the koala. Use the information from the text.

	Panda	Koala
Country		
Colour		
Size		
Food		
Where it lives		

Exercise 4: Read Carefully for Details

Work with a partner. Look in the text for the answers.

1. Why do people like pandas and koalas?

2. Pandas and koalas are bears.   T (true) or F (false)?

3. What parts of the panda are black?

4. When does the koala sleep?

5. Why does the koala have a strange smell?

6. Why are pandas and koalas in danger?

The Camel

Exercise 1: Get Ready to Read

Work with a partner. Discuss these questions.

1. Where do camels live?

2. What do people use them for?

Exercise 2: Read Quickly for General Ideas

The Camel

In very early times, camels lived in the deserts of North America. They moved from there to Asia. Today we don't find camels in North America, but we do find them in the deserts of central Asia, north Africa and Arabia. People in these countries use camels to carry things across the desert. Camels can carry 250-300 kilograms.

The camel is an animal with a large neck, small ears and strong teeth. When it is angry it uses its teeth to bite. The colour of the camel can be white, tan or dark brown. It has long legs and it can travel quickly.

The camel lives in the desert without problems. The animals' feet have thick soles to protect them from the hot sand. Their feet are broad and flat. This helps the camel to walk on the sand. The camel also has a hump on its back. In the rainy season the camel stores food in its hump. Then it can go for days with no food. Finally, the camel has two stomachs. It can fill one stomach with water, so it doesn't need to drink so often.

The camel is sometimes called the ship of the desert. People have used the camel to carry things in the desert for 5000 years. It is also used for food and for making tents, shoes and clothing. The camel is also special because it knows when it is near water. It can smell water!

Exercise 3: Transfer Information

Look at the picture of the camel. Work with a partner to name the parts of the camel's body. Use the information in the text to help you.

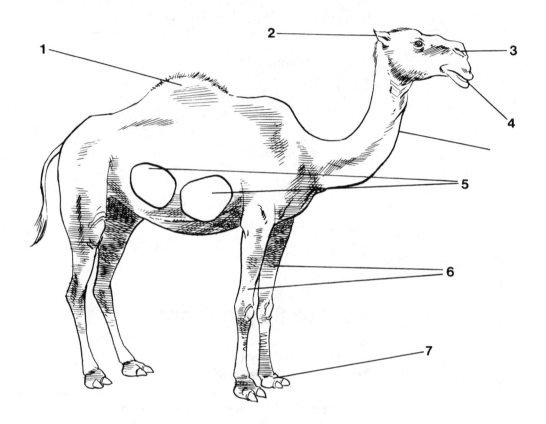

Exercise 4: Read Carefully for Details

Work with a partner. Look in the text for the answers.

1. Where did the first camels live?

2. Where do we find camels today?

3. What do people use camels for?

4. Describe three things about the camel's appearance.

5. When does a camel bite?

6. What colours are camels?

7. Why can a camel travel quickly?

8. What helps a camel walk on the hot sand?

9. What is a camel's hump for?

10. Why doesn't the camel need to drink water in the desert?

11. What is another name people sometimes give the camel?

12. Name some other uses of the camel.

Exercise 5: Practise Spelling

Fill in the missing letters.

d_ _ert

As_a

ne_k

colo_r

sa_d

r_iny

stom_c_

te_t_

How to Buy a Camel

(**Listening Activity 14**)

Exercise 1: Get Ready to Listen

Before you begin, cover Exercise 4 on page 125.

☐☐ Read these questions aloud with a partner.

1. A camel buyer should look for a camel that is:
   a) tall
   b) fat
   c) young

2. A camel's legs should be:
   a) short
   b) strong
   c) soft

3. A camel's skin should be:
   a) brown
   b) white
   c) soft

4. A buyer should be careful because:

   a) a camel is tall

   b) a camel can bite

   c) a camel is friendly

5. A camel should have:

   a) a good family tree

   b) a lot of water

   c) a place to sleep

6. The best place to buy camels is:

   a) in North America

   b) in Saudi Arabia

   c) in central Asia

⊙⊙ Exercise 2: Listen for Meaning

Listen to the conversation. What is the conversation about?

⊙⊙ Exercise 3: Listen for Details

Go back to the questions. While you listen, choose the correct answer.

⊙⊙ Exercise 4: Listen for Sounds

While you listen, write the missing words.

How to Buy a Camel

Tourist: Can you give me some advice please? I want ____ buy a camel. What should I look for?

Camel owner: Look for a tall animal. That'____ important when you buy a camel. A camel should be tall. Tall with strong legs. The best camels have long, strong legs.

Tourist: Hmmm. I see. Anything else?

Camel owner: Yes, of course. Check ____ skin. You want soft skin. Soft skin and also soft fur. The softer the fur is, the better the quality is.

Tourist: Oh yeah? Anything else? Are ____ teeth important?

Camel owner: The teeth? Sure. Check the teeth. But be careful. Camels bite.

Tourist: OK, sure. And the ears?

Camel owner: The ears? Yes, the larger, _____ better. And, finally, the family tree _____ important.

Tourist: The family tree?

Camel owner: Yes. I mean, ask about where the camel comes from. Who are its parents. What region _____ comes from.

Tourist: What region is best?

Camel owner: _____. _ _ _ _. That's the best place for camels. _____ in Saudi Arabia.

Tourist: Thank you. Thanks a lot.

Camel owner: OK. Good luck.

Supplementary Grammar

Subject Pronouns, Object Pronouns

Subject Pronouns

When you refer to someone or something without using the name of the person or thing, you use the pronoun.

Exercise 1

Give the plural form of these pronouns:

1. I
2. you
3. he
4. she
5. it

Exercise 2

Give the pronouns for the following nouns:

1. a student
2. pencil and paper
3. people
4. my brother and I
5. the teacher
6. desks
7. chalk
8. the other teacher
9. the blackboard
10. books

Object Pronouns

Formation

The following chart shows the form of subject pronouns and object pronouns.

I	me
you	you
he	him
she	her
it	it
we	us
you	you
they	them

Usage

An object pronoun can be used as:

   a **direct object**

Example: I know him

   an **indirect object**

Example: We gave her clear directions

   an **object of a preposition**

Example: She explained the subject to us.

Exercise 1

Choose the correct pronoun.

1. (We, us) are classmates.
2. The teacher always speaks to (we, us) in English.
3. That girl lives near (he, him).
4. The teacher divided the papers between (we, us.)
5. I like to talk with (she, her).
6. He explained the exercise to (they, them).
7. Her parents sent (she, her) a letter.
8. (He, him) studies very hard.
9. That student always sits near (I, me).
10. (They, them) are from Taiwan.

Exercise 2

Give the correct pronoun to replace the words in brackets.

1. _____ are late. (Alice and her brother)
2. I gave _____ to him. (the tape recorder)
3. Please write _____ on the paper. (the words)
4. He often sends _____ letters. (his parents)
5. That book is for _____. (my sister)
6. The teacher always speaks to _____ in English. (this class)
7. _____ learn quickly. (the sisters)
8. Sometimes _____ is late for class. (the teacher)
9. His parents send _____ money every month. (the student)
10. I gave _____ to the teacher this morning. (my homework)

How Many, How Much

Some nouns can be counted.

Example: How many:

days, people, dollars, cities?

Some nouns cannot be counted.

Example: How much:

water, time, money, food?

Exercise 1

Complete these questions with **much** or **many**.

1. How _____ money do you need?
2. How _____ hours are banks open every day?
3. How _____ employees work at this bank?
4. How _____ change does he need?
5. How _____ coins does Canada have?
6. How _____ exchange do you get for an American dollar?
7. How _____ tellers are men?
8. How _____ banks do you have in your city?
9. How _____ colours are Canadian bills?
10. How _____ time does it take to cash a cheque?

Exercise 2

Write questions to ask another student about somewhere he or she has lived. Use **how much** and **how many**. Ask about:

1. climate

2. population

3. geographical location

4. transportation

5. tourist attractions

Present Continuous Aspect

Formation

The present continuous aspect uses the auxiliary verb **to be**, and the main verb ends in **-ing**.

Example: We are going.

Usage

The present continuous aspect is for an action in present time. Use it when the action is **in progress** in present time.

Exercise 1

Write the correct form of the auxiliary verb **to be**.

1. I

2. you

3. he

4. she

5. it

6. we

7. you

8. they

Exercise 2

We are watching passengers on the bus. Write the correct auxiliary verb form of **to be** for these sentences.

1. Two women ____ shaking hands.
2. That man ____ carrying a big package.
3. Max ____ reading the newspaper.
4. Tanya and Melissa ____ putting their tickets in the fare box.
5. I ____ ringing the bell.
6. The driver ____ giving transfers to the passengers.
7. The bus ____ moving slowly in traffic.
8. The child ____ holding her mother's hand.
9. We ____ transferring to the subway here.
10. Two passengers ____ asking for directions.
11. The boys ____ getting off at the next bus stop.

Question Form

Yes/No Questions

To make questions in the present continuous, use the auxiliary verb **to be** and then the subject.

Example:

    Statement: He is leaving.

    Question: Is he leaving?

Exercise 1

Build questions from the information you have.

Example:

    going/you: Are you going home after school?

1. eating/they
2. dancing/the other students
3. learning/your friend
4. studying/you
5. listening/they
6. writing/Paula

7. speaking/the teacher

8. stopping/the bus

9. discussing/the group

10. talking/the taxi driver

Exercise 2

Write six **yes/no** questions about actions in the classroom. Use these verbs:

sitting   writing   standing   smiling   listening   speaking

Information Questions

Wh- questions ask for information: **Where? Why? When? What? Who? How** also asks for information.

In an information question, use the question word first: **Where**?

Then use the auxiliary verb: Where **are**?

Then use the subject: Where are **you**?

Finally, use the main verb in the continuous (-ing) form: Where are you **going**?

Exercise 1

Write information questions based on the following statements.

1. I am eating.

2. I am going.

3. I am studying.

4. They are sleeping.

5. They are discussing.

6. I am coming.

7. He is coming

8. We are shouting

9. She is answering.

Exercise 2

Write the correct question word for each sentence.

1. ____ are you eating? A hamburger.
2. ____ are we meeting? At 8 o'clock.
3. ____ is coming? Steve.
4. ____ are they going? To a movie.
5. ____ are you laughing? The movie is funny.
6. ____ is she practising? With a tape recorder.

Negative Form

Formation

To make negative sentences, use the auxiliary verb **to be** and add **not**.

Example:

Affirmative: She is listening.

Negative: He is not listening.

Contractions are often used with negative sentences:

I'm not

you aren't

he isn't

she isn't

it isn't

we aren't

you aren't

they aren't

Exercise 1

Make negative sentences from the words that are given. Use contractions.

Example:

snowing/it: It isn't snowing.

1. stopping/the bus
2. traffic/moving fast
3. sitting/that passenger

4. getting off/I

5. waiting/Max and Millicent

6. crossing the street/My classmates and I

7. changing buses/the passengers

8. leaving the station/the train

9. holding her mother's hand/Andrea

Exercise 2

Write six sentences about things people in the class aren't doing right now.

Present Simple Tense

Negative Form

Formation

Use the auxiliary verb **do** and the word **not** before the main verb. Don't forget that the third person singular form of **do** is **does**.

Contractions are **don't** and **doesn't**.

Exercise 1

Complete these sentences in the negative.

1. Jerry (knows) _____ their names.

2. The teacher (gives) _____ homework very often.

3. I (like) _____ strong coffee.

4. Satomi (comes) _____ from China.

5. People (ride) _____ bicycles in winter in Winnipeg.

6. That student (sleeps) _____ well before exams.

7. We (find) _____ the work very difficult.

8. You (read) _____ that newspaper very often.

9. Mark (wakes up) _____ before 8:30.

10. That man (smiles) _____ much.

Exercise 2

Write negative sentences using these verbs.

1. take
2. understand
3. write
4. smile
5. see
6. eat

Going To

Formation

One way to talk about future time is with the expression **going to**.

Going to is used with the auxiliary verb **to be** before it. **Going to** is followed by the base form of the verb.

Examples:

Charles **is going to** see a movie tonight.

I **am going to** visit my friend after dinner.

You **are going to** love Paris.

He **is going to** play tennis tomorrow.

She **is going to** go to the supermarket tonight.

It **is going to** rain soon.

We **are going to** do our homework.

You **are going to** meet my sister at the dinner.

They **are going to** go home early.

N.B. **Going to** is sometimes pronounced "gonna."

Usage

Going to is an expression used to describe future time. **Going to** is used to suggest future plans or intentions.

Exercise 1

Fill in the correct auxiliary verb form (**am**, **is** or **are**) and **going to**. Match the person or thing on the left with the activity on the right.

1. The captain of the team ____   exercise in the park.

2. The weather ____   lend me her tennis racket.

3. Mr. Lin ____   put on my skis.

4. The hockey player ____   win the race.

5. You and Tom ____   protect the players.

6. The skiers ____   ask for time out.

7. Gaby and I ____   change to rain.

8. You ____   practise in the pool.

9. My friend ____   wear warm hats.

10. I ____   put on his skates.

11. The equipment ____   carry the equipment.

12. The swim team ____   eat after we play.

Exercise 2

Make sentences with **going to**.

1. Tara/learn to skate

2. Hiroshi/teach judo

3. The best team/win the Stanley Cup

4. The new snow/help the skiers

5. I/exercise at the gym

6. Jeannot and Madelyne/bring their tennis rackets

7. Annabel and I/meet at the pool

8. Gaby/wear warm clothes

9. John and Howard/join the team

10. My grandmother/teach me tai chi

Exercise 3

Write five sentences about things you are going to do later today. Write three sentences about things you are going to do in the next five years.

Question Form

To make a question use the subject and the auxiliary verb **to be**.

Example:

Statement: Our team is going to win.

Question: Is our team going to win?

Exercise 1

Change these statements to questions.

1. Germany is going to win the swimming competition.
2. The French and Canadian teams are going to work hard.
3. The Olympic Games are going to be in Atlanta.
4. I am going to like judo.
5. The weather is going to be good for sailing.
6. My skates are going to be comfortable for you.

Exercise 2

Make questions with **going to**:

1. You/meet us at the pool
2. Steve/join the team
3. My sister/learn to play tennis
4. Our team/win the game
5. You and Ping/know how to skate
6. Those girls/carry the equipment into the gym
7. I/like tai chi
8. Ursula and I/be good tennis partners
9. The hockey player/be ready for the game
10. Americans/play baseball in winter

Exercise 3

Ask about your friends' plans for the weekend. Make five questions with **going to**.

Negative Form

To use **going to** in the negative, make the auxiliary verb **to be** negative by adding **not**.

Example:

Affirmative: We are going to play tennis.

Negative: We are not going to play tennis.

Exercise 1

Write five sentences about some things you are **not** going to do later today.

Exercise 2

Make a chart similar to the one below. Ask three students in the class about activities they plan to do next week. Write their names and write "yes" or "no" for each one.

Names			
Go to a restaurant			
Visit friends			
Call home			
See a movie			
Practise a sport			
Go to the bank			
Watch TV			
Visit another city			
Do homework			
Write a letter			
Go skiing			
Ride a bike			

Now write ten sentences about your classmates' plans. Use the answers to the questions above.

Comparison of Adjectives

Comparative -er Form

Formation

When adjectives have one syllable, add **-er** to form the comparative.

    Example: old   older

When adjectives have two syllables and they end in **y**, change **y** to **i** and add **-er**.

    Example: easy   easier

Exceptions (irregular forms):

good	better
bad	worse
far	farther

Exercise 1

Write the comparative forms of these adjectives.

1. low
2. tidy
3. fancy
4. short
5. kind
6. far
7. early
8. high
9. loud
10. bad
11. funny
12. wide
13. good
14. hard
15. strong

Exercise 2

Write the comparative form of the missing words.

1. The weather in Canada is ____ than in the United States. (cold)

2. Some students came to class ____ than other students. (early)

3. Sandra is ____ than Gaby. (tall)

4. The subway is ____ than the bus. (fast)

5. Movies are ____ on Tuesday than on Saturday. (cheap)

6. Jason's accident was ____ than Ray's accident. (bad)

7. Prices at Eaton's are ____ than prices at Holt. (low)

8. Tokyo is ____ than Alaska. (far)

9. Rock and roll is usually ____ than folk music. (loud)

Superlative -est Form

Formation

When adjectives have one syllable, add **-est** to form the comparative.

    Example: young   youngest

When adjectives have two syllables and they end in **y**, change **y** to **i** and add **-est**.

    Example: sunny   sunniest

Exceptions:

good	better	best
bad	worse	worst
far	farther	farthest

Exercise 1

Choose the best comparative word.

1. Hamburgers are the ____ meal. (highest, fastest, biggest)

2. For many people, hamburgers have the ____ taste. (strongest, best, worst)

3. Hamburgers with relish make the ____ meal. (fastest, tastiest, coldest)

4. We ate at the table that was ____ from the door. (farthest, fattest, best)

5. Hamburgers are not the ____ fast food. (oldest, youngest, newest)

6. Milk-shakes are the ____ drinks. (funniest, sweetest, hottest)

7. Mexican food is the ____ food. (coldest, spiciest, highest)

Rule for Pronunciation and Spelling

If you add a vowel to a word with one syllable, the sound may change. The short vowel becomes a long vowel.

Examples:

plan	plane
pin	pine
hop	hope
cut	cute
pet	Pete

To add an ending (such as **-er**) without changing the sound, double the last letter.

Example: big   bigger   biggest

Exercise 1

Give the correct spelling for the following words in comparative form.

1. tall
2. hot
3. old
4. thin
5. fat
6. low
7. wet
8. fast
9. slim
10. blue
11. red
12. long
13. sad
14. big
15. wide

Exercise 2

Put these words in alphabetical order. Then write the comparative form.

new   blue   hard   short   small   late   sad   young   fast   slow   strong   old   long   big

Exercise 3

Write sentences using comparisons with these words:

1. coffee/hot

2. waiter/fast

3. plate/small

4. restaurant/old

5. tips/big

6. dessert/sweet

7. music/loud

Exercise 4

Write the words your teacher spells. Then write the continuous form of the verb (**-ing**) next to each one. Be careful to apply the rule about short and long vowels.

Example: sit   sitting

Exercise 5

Work with a partner. Use the rule about short and long vowels to say these words aloud.

1. slime	11. tipping
2. grim	12. mat
3. written	13. butter
4. cute	14. rate
5. showing	15. cod
6. hop	16. set
7. lip	17. plate
8. pane	18. code
9. site	19. shade
10. hate	20. cake

Irregular Past Tense Forms

become	became
begin	began
bring	brought
build	built
buy	bought
come	came
cost	cost
cut	cut
drink	drank
eat	ate
fall	fell
feel	felt
find	found
forget	forgot
give	gave
go	went
get	got
grow	grew
have	had
hear	heard
know	knew
leave	left
lose	lost
make	made
pay	paid
put	put
read	read*
ride	rode
run	ran
see	saw
sell	sold
send	sent

*Note that the pronunciation changes in the past tense to "red."

sit	sat
sleep	slept
speak	spoke
take	took
teach	taught
tell	told
think	thought
understand	understood
wear	wore
write	wrote

Contractions

To Be

I am	I'm		we are	we're
you are	you're		you are	you're
he is	he's		they are	they're
she is	she's			
it is	it's			

Negative Form

I am not	I'm not		we are not	we aren't
you are not	you aren't		you are not	you aren't
he is not	he isn't		they are not	they aren't
she is not	she isn't			
it is not	it isn't			

Past Tense

I was not	I wasn't		we were not	we weren't
you were not	you weren't		you were not	you weren't
he was not	he wasn't		they were not	they weren't
she was not	she wasn't			
it was not	it wasn't			

Do Not

I do not	I don't		we do not	we don't
you do not	you don't		you do not	you don't
she does not	she doesn't		they do not	they don't
he does not	he doesn't			
it does not	it doesn't			

Cannot

I cannot	I can't		we cannot	we can't
you cannot	you can't		you cannot	you can't
he cannot	he can't		they cannot	they can't
she cannot	she can't			
it cannot	it can't			

Community Contact Tasks

In the Community

Task #1

Buying a Coat

You need to buy a new coat. Go to a clothing store or the clothing department of a department store. Choose a coat. (Don't buy it.)

Describe the coat you chose. Be sure to give the following information:

Type of coat (winter coat, spring coat, jacket, raincoat)

Colour

Size

Price

Number of buttons

Number of pockets

Does it have:

a lining?

a hood?

a zipper?

a belt?

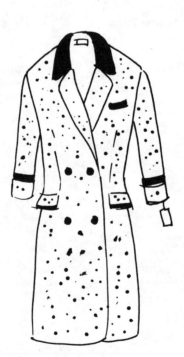

In the Community

Task #2

Using Change

These are some things that we need exact change to do:

Use a public phone

Take a city bus

Buy a newspaper on the street

Use a vending machine

Park at a parking meter

Use a washing machine

Buy stamps at a stamp machine

Find the information to complete this chart.

	Total Cost	**Change Needed**
Public Phone	.25	1 × 25¢ 2 × 10¢ + 1 × 5¢
Bus		
Newspaper		
Vending machine		
Parking meter		
Washing machine		
Stamp machine		

In the Community

Task #3

Outside Workers

Go for a walk and make a list of people you see at work. Write down five jobs you see. Then complete this chart.

Job	Where	Uniform: Yes/No
police officer	in a car	yes
1.		
2.		
3.		
4.		
5.		

In the Community

Task #4

International Lunch

Bring in food that your family eats at home. Write the name of the food and the main ingredients on a card. Put the card beside the food. Everyone gets to taste different kinds of food.

First make a chart to plan what each student in the class will bring.

Name of Student	Main Course	Dessert	Drink	Other
Maria	Lasagna			
Ali			Coca-Cola	

In the Community

Task #5

The Bread Task

Go to a store that sells bread in your neighbourhood. Find four different kinds of bread or rolls. Then answer the questions.

1. Where did you go?

   a) a bakery   c) a grocery store

   b) a supermarket   d) other

2. What was the name of the store?

3. What were the names of the breads you found?

   a) white sliced   g) French bread

   b) rye bread   h) bagel

   c) corn bread   i) rolls

   d) pumpernickel   j) pita

   e) whole wheat   k) other

   f) oatmeal

4. How much did the bread or package cost?

   a) less than $1.00   c) more than $1.50

   b) more than $1.00   d) more than $2.00

5. The bread was:

   a) on a shelf   d) in a box

   b) on a counter   e) in a basket

   c) in a bag   f) other

6. How do you eat your bread?

   a) warmed in the oven   c) sliced

   b) toasted   d) as it is

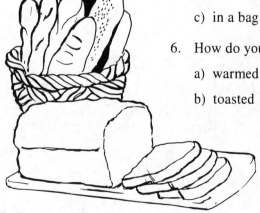

In the Community

Task #6

The Department Store Task

Go to a department store. On the chart, fill in three things you can buy in each department. Give the prices.

	Things You Find	Price
Household Furnishings	e.g., towel	$7.95
Shoes	e.g., slippers	
Toys	e.g., teddy bear	
Sports	e.g., tennis racket	

In the Community

Task #7

The Restaurant Task

A. Go to a restaurant where the menu is posted **outside**. Decide what you want to eat for dinner. Write the names of the things you choose and the prices on the chart. You don't need to go inside.

MENU

Fish	8.95
BBQ Chicken	5.95
Spaghettti	6.35
Soup	1.75
Coffee	.70
Tea	.70

	Name of Food	Price
Entrée		
Main course		
Dessert		
Coffee		

B. Go to a fast-food restaurant. Find five things you want to eat. Write their names and the prices on the chart.

Food or Drink	Price
1.	
2.	
3.	
4.	
5.	

Englisch ist einfach

私は英語が好きです。　اللغة الإنجليزية سهلة

Vaya suka buku ini

Bu Kitapi cok scudim

我會說英文

See you in Canadian Concepts 4!

ণেক্স তুমি

Mi piace molto questo libro

Tôi thích quyển sách này

Inglês é fácil de aprender.

Je parle l'anglais

안녕

Mɪʃaʊ ɛʒʒuⅷⅷá

さようなら

私は、この本から
たくさんの英語を学びました。

Me gusta este libro